The Mind of
PAKISTAN

Attention Authors

Manas Publications is fighting a war to tell the world that India can win the battle not only by the bullet but also by the pen. We are converting fighters into writers. There is no dearth of intellectuals in our country, however, their knowledge is confined to them only. No sincere effort has been made by any other publisher to give the right direction to their knowledge and the talent of every intellectual is lying hidden. An author always presents the raw material in the shape of a manuscript and it is the job of the publisher to convert it to a finished product. Manas has been continually motivating intellectuals and publishing their manuscripts for more than two decades and would like to publish your manuscript too. If you or your colleagues have a manuscript ready for publication or are working on it, contact us with a detailed synopsis and list of contents. Manas will also suggest you a suitable title for writing related to your area of expertise. Manas is known for its publishing quality. We take utmost care in publishing and also give wide publicity to the book and its author through our national and international distribution network.

The Mind of
PAKISTAN

Kishori Lal
Former Indian Diplomat

Manas Publications
New Delhi-110002 (INDIA)

MANAS PUBLICATIONS

(We Convert Fighters into Writers)

(Publishers, Library Suppliers, Importers & Exporters)

4402/5-A, Ansari Road (Opp. HDFC Bank)
Darya Ganj, New Delhi-110 002 (India)
Off. (23260783, 23265523, Fax: 011-23272766
E-mail: manaspublications@vsnl.com
manaspublications@gmail.com

ISBN 978-81-7049-345-7

₹ 495/-

Designed at

Manas Publications

Printed in India at
HS Offsets, Delhi
and published by Mrs Suman Lata for
Manas Publications, 4402/5-A,
Ansari Road, (Opp. HDFC Bank),
Darya Ganj, New Delhi-110 002 (INDIA)

Preface

A day before I left New Delhi I was aware of the tension slowly building up between India and Pakistan. When I was posted to Karachi a month before, I was supposed to go with my family, that is, my wife and two sons. In preparation, I withdrew my sons from the school and started packing up, when I was suddenly advised by the Ministry not to take my family with me. The Ministry could have stopped me too, but that did not happen. Later on arrival in Karachi I learnt that the person I was to relieve, a South Indian, had been for some time clamouring to go back home. So, I had to go alone. It was a common practice in our circle that not every one liked to go to Pakistan. Some had haunting memories of the partition and some were psychologically afraid of going to Pakistan from where the Hindus and the Sikhs were driven out with blood marks on their foreheads instead of the traditional vermilion mark. Whenever a meeting of the committee handling postings abroad was held, many approached senior officers with a request not to be posted to Pakistan. When I accepted the transfer without any grumble, some of my colleagues thought I was a fool.

Since I was born in Pakistan (part of undivided India then) and had lived there for eighteen years before my family migrated to India in the wake of the partition without losing any member or being attacked by the Muslims, I did not have any fear and misapprehension of going to Pakistan. My father and my elder brothers had many Muslim friends and I had a few besides many classmates. It was a shared practice to exchange greetings and even cooked dishes on festive occasions of each community. We did not have any feeling of animosity other than what is generally apparent in business and profession in the same way as is between two persons belonging to the same religion and community. As a matter of fact creation of Pakistan came as sad news to us and we thought those Hindus living in Pakistan as a minority might not have the same privileges that they enjoyed in undivided India. Nobody by any stretch of imagination could think of mass migration - the Hindus living in Pakistan migrating to India and the Muslims living in India migrating to Pakistan.

Events took such a dramatic ugly turn causing bloodshed, besides arson and looting, that the Hindus had no time to plan their move. Most of them had to leave all their liquid assets - cash and ornaments and even their clothes and utensils behind. But, as I have said, because no harm was dome to our family, I did not have haunting memories of the partition as most of the migrants had. I did not give even a second thought to my posting. In fact, as the Ministry was seized of the fluid political situation in Pakistan, my request for cancellation of the transfer might have received sympathetic consideration. I did not try. Of course, I had a personal desire too. I wanted to take advantage of my posting to Karachi to go to my native place Muzaffargarh, near Multan in the Punjab. I loved the place where I was born. Thinly populated, it had much of free land - a desert on one side while amazingly fertile lush green land on the other side (that did dry up to some extent during summer), just six miles on the west bank of the river Chenab. I wanted to have a feel of the place so well known for juicy mangoes and dates of a large variety. It is a different story that my desire was not fulfilled because the Government of Pakistan did not permit any of our people to go out of Karachi. Besides, the climate was not conducive to undertake a trip by train to a place about 300 miles away from

Karachi. I might have ventured a trip by air, if the Government of Pakistan had given me the permission.

When I reached Karachi, it was before noon. An official from the Indian Mission came to receive me and took me straight to the house allotted to me. In fact it was a large house that was shared by another colleague of mine, Sushil Chandra. He too had come without family and we shared the kitchen too. A Bengali Muslim servant cooked the food. He was a good cook but being very young he slept late at night and was in the habit of getting up late in the morning. We had to take our breakfast hurriedly so as to reach the office in time. But in any case pestered by the Pakistan intelligence he left us after three months and we could not find a replacement. Nobody was prepared to work with us for fear of the police and the intelligence. We had to request one of our lower staff members to cook for us. Since I had served earlier for two years (November 58 to January 61) in Dacca (East Pakistan) that had a large contingent of personnel from India, I knew many families and a few of them were there in Karachi. Occasionally, they invited me for parties and dinners that to some extent relieved me of much boredom and loneliness. For reasons of security, the High Commission rented big large complexes to put many families in the same building. Once a while on weekend we went to Clifton beach where we had our own hut. The house where Sushil Chandra and I lived was, in fact, a huge building that was constructed and owned by the High Commission at a time when the High Commissioner had not yet moved to Islamabad. It was initially intended for officers of the rank of First Secretary, but as many officers moved to Islamabad, the building became vacant and that is how I went there. While Sushil Chandra had his bedroom at one end, I had at another end. Often we joked that if someone needed call another in an emergency, even if he shouted at the top of his voice, his call would not reach the other end. Why the Government of India on the recommendation of the earlier High Commissioner, an ICS Officer, provided such big accommodation to a First Secretary (equivalent to the rank of a Deputy Secretary back at home), had more a sort of status symbol than actual need. The idea perhaps was to project the bigness of India - a false notion, of course, at that time (in the fifties), when India was still struggling to stand on her economically week legs.

Karachi, though no longer the capital of Pakistan was nevertheless an important city and a port comparable to Bombay. When I landed in the morning I did not see any abnormal activity. The main stream of life in general seemed to be running smoothly irrespective of what was happening in East Pakistan (East Bengal). Perhaps it was too early for me to make any assessment but gradually I found that the manner in which the Government of Pakistan had woefully kept the masses in West Pakistan ignorant of happenings in East Bengal was remarkable. There was total censorship of news. All the newspapers almost carried the identical stories and there was hardly any column spared for any news from foreign press. The quality of the newspapers (DAWN and MORNING NEWS in English) was still poor. The Urdu newspapers though did often carry news not covered by the English papers and the standard of their editorials was better, obviously because Urdu papers had a much larger readership and had some old Editors who could better express themselves in the native language than in English.

Contents

Introduction

A spate of terrorist attacks in recent years by Islamic fundamentalists erupting like a volcano with its epicenter in Pakistan suddenly reminded me of the diary I had maintained when I was working as Visa Attaché with the Assistant High Commissioner of India in Karachi in 1971.

I joined the Commission in April 71 and returned to Delhi in November 71, a few days before the Indo-Pakistan War (December 3 to 14, 71) broke out. I was the last officer from the Ministry of External Affairs to be sent to Pakistan. Nobody was posted after me in 1971. The Ministry had sensed the trouble and hence all postings to Pakistan were temporarily frozen. On arrival at a new place of posting, it is customary to call on the Head of the Mission. In Karachi he was called the Assistant High Commissioner (AHC) as the High Commissioner was stationed in Islamabad, the capital of Pakistan. The AHC, K.N. Bakshi, a young, energetic and enterprising IFS officer, on my first meeting, after exchange of usual pleasantries, asked me a straightforward question: could I collect information from the Pakistanis who came to apply for visas to India? I had not worked with him before. As a matter of fact I met him for the first time, though I was familiar with his name. That type of work, that is, gathering intelligence through the public or more precisely from men and women desirous of visiting India usually for the purpose of meeting their relatives and friends, was customarily meant for officers from the intelligence service. As I had no experience of extracting sensitive information from the general public and I had also no training in this field, I told him I would have to think over it. Though I was keen to undertake this type of challenging work, I thought I had to mull over the matter before giving him a reply. The subject occupied my mind for two days. I should figure out how I was going to do it. After considerable thought I accepted the challenge and told him that I would try my best to get as much information as possible. He was apparently pleased at my reply but he did not ask me how I would work on that. Perhaps, he had his own way of judging things or he was not sure of my ability to deliver the goods.

I had about twenty people working under me. Since the number of Pakistanis visiting India was quite substantial and the number of applications received on any working day, on an average, was about three hundred, we had a large Visa Office to carefully scrutinize each application before issuing the visa. In the wake of the partition almost every Muslim family in India had relations in Pakistan and vice versa. In fact, for economic or political reasons, many Muslim families in India bifurcated themselves in order to have one leg in India and the other in Pakistan or in other words to have best of both the worlds, if possible. Of course, for the last three or four months as tension between India and Pakistan was mounting, the number of applications had dwindled to less than a hundred a day.

I, therefore, instructed my staff to place all the visa applications on my table irrespective of the fact whether the applicant was entitled to a visa or not, or whether the case required a clearance from the Headquarters (the Ministries of External Affairs and Home Affairs). I went through each application, some hurriedly and some very carefully, using partly my own judgement and partly relying on my intuition. From the lot I selected a few. I called some of the applicants for interview whom I considered useful, that is, those who could give me some information on the happenings in Pakistan. I did gather some fruitful tips from many of them. That was one very productive source of my information. Of course, I did not retain the names of the visitors in my diary for security reasons. I was afraid if by any chance my diary fell into the hands of the Pakistan Government, the persons who gave me the information would be in trouble. Of course, while recording my observations, I did give the names to the AHC. (There is no doubt that I now regret not having kept their names for authenticity).

Many applicants were surely aware of the fact that the information given by them would be passed on to India. Some of them, desperate to get the visa, did give out something or the other on my word that their names would not be disclosed. Using his own common sense and his own knowledge of the affairs in Pakistan from his own sources, the AHC heavily relied on my notes for their authenticity and utility. But in order to demonstrate his own ability and intelligence, he did not pass on original notes recorded by me to the Ministry, nor did he mention my name anywhere. He copiously used them for sending his confidential reports to the Ministry. That was his job. I had no say. I had no grouse. After all, he was my boss and I depended on his goodwill for my confidential reports – a must for my next promotion. In India, at least, it is common for officers to take credit for the work done by those who report to them. Perhaps elsewhere too this is how the model works.

All the information the visa seekers gave to me was not useful and some was concocted to win my sympathy so that I might sanction a visa without any huff and hassle. But I took great care in distilling. Much of the extract came handy to me in comprehending the mind of Pakistan and the mind of the military regime. For example, at least four persons told me unambiguously that preparations for war against India were going on. One person went to the extent of disclosing to me that all leave to military personnel had been cancelled and even the ex-servicemen were being recalled to duty. Pakistan was determined to attack India, I concluded, as more and more facts came to my knowledge. Of course, I was not the sole source of eliciting this kind of information. Every Government has her own sources and the Government of India could not be an exception. But when reports coming from different sources corroborate one another in essential details, each report stands on its own merit and any report at that critical juncture coming from the High Commission had an intrinsic value.

One marked difference, however, I noticed in the temperament of the visitors. The Muslims who had migrated from the North of India especially from the U.P. and Delhi were less cooperative and sometimes even reluctant to tell anything. Ironically it is the Muslims from these parts of India that had been more vociferous in demanding a separate homeland for Muslims. Whether they had a guilty conscience after watching the high drama of intrigue and mutual bickering among the Muslim brethren migrating to Pakistan right from its very inception or they were more secretive, I cannot say. But I never tried to put pressure on anyone or say in clear words that granting of a visa was subject to furnishing of sensitive materials. It is a different matter if the visitor knowing well that I had the full authority to grant a visa, in order to get my nod, came forward of his own free will. I think many of them, desperate to visit India to meet their relatives, most of them very close, did provide some crucial facts.

It is a common belief that in any kind of war the soldiers die, but the credit for victory goes to the Generals. In civil service the people at the lower level do the spadework, but the credit goes to the Secretaries, the Directors and the Ambassadors. That is the system, though in all fairness I must say in the event of defeat or loss of face, the blame falls on the Generals, who become answerable both to the Government and the people. In civil service the civilian Generals under cloud or condemned for inefficiency are usually transferred to unimportant departments and in foreign service to small insignificant posts abroad as a punishment, though in reality it happens once a while. Under the rules it is virtually impossible to dismiss a civil servant. I am giving this analogy to highlight the fact that though much of the information given by me to the AHC was used by him in sending dispatches to the Ministry, all the credit went to him. Once perhaps in a generous mood, he frankly admitted to me after the war when we happened to meet in the corridor of the South Block, the permanent headquarters of the Ministry of External Affairs, that the Ministry had told him the reports sent by him were more authentic than the those sent by the High Commissioner in Islamabad. He acknowledged that he extensively used the notes prepared by me.

I retained much of the information in my diary. Interestingly the Office of the Deputy High Commissioner for India in Dacca was closed two to three months before the war. Any person in East Pakistan wanting a visa for India had to come all the way to Karachi. That is how it became possible to get inside news of happenings and events in East Pakistan. Most of the visa seekers were non-Bengali Muslims working in East Pakistan, usually as small businessmen and in Government service, who had their relatives spread all over India. Though the Bengali Muslims had also their relatives and fiends in West Bengal, they were reluctant to come to West Pakistan because of the hostile attitude of non-Bengalis, particularly, the Punjabi Muslims towards them and the cold war of mistrust bordering on covert hostility between the two wings of Pakistan.

My second source of information that helped me in welding broken pieces of facts given by the visa seekers was the newspapers and magazines both in English and Urdu. The Urdu papers gave more news of local events and unrest in Pakistan because that was (and still is) the main language understood and spoken in West Pakistan, more so in Karachi which has a large population of Muslims who had migrated from India at the time of partition and even in the following years. Since I was born and brought up and received my school education in Muzaffargarh, a small town at that time, twentyone miles west of Multan, I had a fair background of the typography of the country and a good knowledge of the customs among Muslims, mostly gathered from books in Urdu language and from my elders. Personal experience, I must confess was limited, because when I migrated to India with my family I was just eighteen and had passed my matriculation. Still it was not so difficult for me to understand what was going on in the minds of the people. And as my early education was in Urdu (Hindi was almost unknown then) I had no difficulty in reading Urdu newspapers and in translating relevant material into English. Incidentally, translating from English to Urdu and vice versa was a part of the school curriculum.

The tension between India and Pakistan had started building up from March 1971 when Mujib-ur-Rehman, the acknowledged leader of the Bengalis, who was in absolute majority in East Pakistan, declared independence and he named it Bangla Desh. Mujib was undoubtedly a very popular leader and had the support of more than 90% of the population of East Pakistan. His declaration of independence for East Pakistan created turmoil among the political bosses and the military brass in Pakistan. They were naturally perturbed because they knew that Mujib had the full backing of Indira Gandhi, the then Prime Minister of India. It would have been a Herculean task for the military junta to woo India whom they had viciously antagonized because of their overt designs on Kashmir. But perhaps they did not get panicky because they had the full moral and military support of the United States of America and full backing of China. They must have concluded that India was no match to the combined strength of the USA and China. No wonder in 1965 war with India the then General Ayub Khan had boasted that with the Patton Tanks supplied by America, the Pakistan Army would walk over Delhi.

The Government of Pakistan put restrictions on our movements out of Karachi for their security considerations. India, as a precautionary measure, restricted the issue of visas to Pakistanis because New Delhi had sensed the trouble that was brewing up. India had legitimate fears that Pakistan would push men from their Armed Forces and Intelligence Service into India in the garb of the visitors. There was practically no trade between the two countries and no cultural exchanges. All these things resulted in considerably reducing the workload in Karachi Mission and in fact in the last two months before the war there was almost no work to do. But it was not a Roman holiday. The mental pressure of living in a hostile country preparing for war was building up. We could not go anywhere for recreation. The Ministry of External Affairs might have anticipated reduced work in the Mission, but to withdraw some officers and the staff all of a sudden might have created a wrong impression in the world that India was contemplating invasion of Pakistan.

Every day at about eleven all diplomatic officers stationed in Karachi used to meet over a cup of tea in the room adjoining to the office of the AHC and talk about happenings and the rapid turn of events in Pakistan. Some information, recorded in my diary, I must acknowledge, also came from the mouths of two officers from Indian Intelligence. I never bothered and of course, never asked them the source of their quota of news but it did help me a lot in corroborating some of the facts that I had gathered through my sources. These two officers senior to me both in length of service and rank, whenever they spoke, disclosed very little. But nevertheless, they did on occasions blurt out something that had some merit and worth. They reported everything direct to their Head Office in the Ministry of Home Affairs in New Delhi. The AHC was, of course, not happy with them as he thought his work got marginalized. He tried his best to elicit some information from them, but he did not have much success. Had he got any tips from them, it is quite possible he might not have heavily leaned on my services. I think the AHC, a direct recruit to Indian Foreign Service with traces of boyish looks loved to hear his own voice rather than listening to others. He had not yet acquired sufficient maturity and gained much experience to be tactful. Obviously, he lacked the knack to extract useful information from the two Intelligence Officers.

The recordings in my diary are correct and true, though as I have mentioned above, for security reasons, I could not enter the sources of information except those coming from the newspapers and the magazines. I have not made any factual changes. The changes, wherever made, are of editing only. While going through the diary I myself was surprised to notice that every Pakistani military regime has, to my mind, the same philosophy, that is, to remain in power by keeping the citizens of Pakistan in good humour through promises of return to democracy and better governance. But it is also a fact that no military ruler has ever succeeded in the long run in achieving his loudly proclaimed objective of peace and prosperity in the country that would be free from corruption and nepotism. In course of time he gets intoxicated with the unlimited and absolute power that he acquired with show of strength and that intoxication lasts till he lasts.

Judging from the facts gathered from diverse sources, there was hardly any doubt in the minds of my colleagues stationed in Karachi and Islamabad that war between India and Pakistan was not only most likely but also imminent. It appears that Yahya Khan was caught on the wrong foot and could not think rationally of the consequences of war. The latest arms and equipment supplied by the United States of America and China emboldened the military regime to humble and humiliate India. They gambled that even if they lost East Pakistan, they would get that part of Kashmir, which was with India. They had been harping on Kashmir since the creation of Pakistan. They had promised Kashmir both to the dissidents in Indian Kashmir and their own people in Pakistan. Almost every leader in Pakistan, civilian or military, had very often boasted of wresting Kashmir from the clutches of India. They seemed to be so sure of their victory that they underestimated India's strength. This reminds me of what Kasam Rizvi, the leader of the conservative Muslims in Hyderabad before it merged with India, once said about the Hindus of India: "They drink the urine of cows, while we eat cows. They are cowards. How can they fight against us?" The analogy was apparent. While the Muslims were strong because they ate meat, the Hindus were weak because they drank urine.

Before the partition of India that perhaps was the sentiment of many fanatic Muslims, which they probably carried with them when they preferred Pakistan to India. Rizvi himself fled to Pakistan soon after Hyderabad was absorbed into India. Pakistan still talks of Gauris and Gaznis – the Muslim invaders, who first invaded India about thousand years ago for loot, murder and spread of.Islam with sword of which Pakistan, among all the Muslim countries in the world, even today is so proud. Paradoxically more than ninety percent Muslims were converts from Hinduism. The impact of Islam through fear generated by the drawn swords, shining and sharpened with fanatic zeal on the black stone of the Kaba, was so strong that they forgot their roots. Not only that, they even ridiculed those gods and goddesses which they once worshipped so diligently and devotionally. These are the paradoxes of life that perhaps nobody can explain.

Pakistan's over-confidence in her prowess stemmed more from the thorns and thistles of decadent history rather than from the realities of the modern age. Every nation has the right to concoct history and so has Pakistan. And that was what Pakistan did. They changed even the course of History trying to project the beginnings of Pakistan and to that end, the beginnings of Islam from times immemorial when man had no religion and no geography. There were no historians, worth the name, among Muslims in pre-partition days, particularly in those parts that now comprise Pakistan. How historians suddenly emerged on the soil of Pakistan in a short span of less than twenty years is itself a feat of history. It may be worth mentioning that for historical reasons, that is, frequent invasions from the North through Hindukush Mountains, life in the provinces of the North was never settled. There were no educational institutions of the standard that existed in the other parts of India (South, West and East) and naturally there were no intellectuals and historians of any caliber from the North of India (The Punjab, Sind, Baluchistan and NWFP), who could have first hand knowledge of the region to even comment on the history books available to the school and college boys and the general readers. While the Punjab and the Sind provinces had the privilege of having very good writers of fiction, that is, novels, short stories and poetry and books on Religion and ancient mythology, there were no thinkers, philosophers and intellectuals. The only University called the Punjab University located at Lahore had hardly any courses on philosophy, politics, economics, psychology, anthropology and metaphysics. There was no curriculum even for research in the history of the region.

Most of the Muslims in Pakistan, though enjoying the fruits of modern science through electrical gadgets or medicines or even watching western films of semi-nude women, still think of old Islam musing over its deep-rooted conservatism and orthodoxy. The unseen, indirectly heard from the mouths of the so-called custodians of religion and gathered from books with inexplicable, some half scholarly and some paranoiac interpolations made by editors, compilers and the interpreters, some educated and some semi-educated while a few relying on intuition and hearsay lures the raw mind to blind faith or as Coleridge said, "willing suspension of disbelief" or as Keats said, "Heard melodies are sweet but those unheard are sweeter." The mind gets conditioned particularly when a person gets addicted to religious mania at a tender age.

During my seven months stay in Karachi I came to India six times on courier duty bringing the diplomatic bag to Delhi and taking the diplomatic bag from Delhi to Karachi next day. It is strange I did not notice any undue concern and anxiety among my people in India as if they did not anticipate any war or were confident of repelling any attack. The Government of India, unlike the military regime in Pakistan, had made no conscious effort to whip up war hysteria. In fact, many people would not believe me when I said that war was likely in near future. I could not convince them how insecure and uncomfortable we felt in Pakistan. When the plane took off from Delhi airport I had every time an uneasy feeling as though I was going to serve another term in a prison. I do not know the sentiments of a prisoner-of-war when in enemy custody, but I do know my sentiments. I was neither free nor confined to the fourwalls of a prison. I lived in a vacuum. While most of my colleagues had their families with them, I lived almost alone in a big building owned and built by the Government of India when Karachi was the capital of Pakistan. I shared the accommodation with another single officer. We had a Muslim cook, who originated from East Pakistan. But after some time, out of fear, he left us. We had to rely on the Indian peon for our cooking.

My interaction with people, usually those who came to get a visa for India, also revealed both the tragic and human side of mankind. Life was not all hatred, if it was not all love. Sometimes I wondered who had created barriers between man and man and sown the seeds of discord along with the seeds of love. Was man accountable for the woes of his own life or that of another man's life or did God design and ordain mankind that way? People say Satan or Evil is responsible for all the ills and miseries of life. That may be true, but who created Satan or Evil? Some great philosopher or a theologian may be able to throw light on the subject, but all along in my life I have groped for an answer. Refusal or grant of visa made so much difference to the man who came with high hopes of visiting his close relative or a friend in India. I really felt sorry for the man who was refused visa for whatever reason. Many of such persons might have cursed me for rejecting their applications and I might have made some error of judgement somewhere, but I had to do my duty – pleasant or unpleasant. Though I kept no records of the visitors, I still remember a few interesting episodes. These have long been buried in the recesses of my mind.

A Muslim couple who had originally migrated to Pakistan from Hyderabad came to see me for a visa for visiting their native place. The woman tall and beautiful was wearing an Indian sari. She said: "Many Muslims in my neighbourhood object to my wearing a sari. But how can I discard it? I was born and bred in Indian culture. The circumstances forced us to migrate to Pakistan, but my heart is still in India". People aware of the pre-partition history will remember that Hindus constituted 90% population of Hyderabad though it was ruled by the Nizam, a Muslim. No wonder Hindu culture had a considerable influence on the lifestyle of the Muslims just as the Muslim culture had a great influence on the Hindus living in West Punjab where the Hindus were in minority. They seemed to be genuine visitors and had been to India before. I believed them and granted them visa and they went to India. After spending a month or so in Hyderabad they returned to Pakistan. They came again to thank me for the grant of visa. They said that they had enjoyed their visit and were received well by their old friends and even acquaintances. As a gesture of goodwill they offered me a pan (betel leaf – a precious commodity in West Pakistan) which they had brought from India. They wanted to invite me to their house for a dinner but I politely declined their invitation more for their sake than for my own. I was afraid if I visited their house the Pakistan intelligence was sure to question them and perhaps make their life miserable.

Once one of my staff members was arguing with a Muslim woman in burqua. He was insisting on seeing her face because he wanted to compare it with her photo on the application. She was reluctant. I went to the counter and explained to her through the window that it was necessary to check if she was the same woman whose photo was on the application. I told her she would also have to reveal her identity to the Immigration in India. I asked her why she was so hesitant here. Without saying a single word she lifted the veil from her face and said lustily: "Look! You can look as long as you want until you are satisfied." Then suddenly she asked me in good humour: "Do you want to see more of me? I can oblige you." I just smiled.

A young Pakistani Muslim was married to a Muslim girl in India. She had gone to see her parents and had not returned despite many letters written by him. He applied for a visa to visit India. I told him that unless he gave some documentary proof of his marriage and the details of his in-laws, I could not issue a visa immediately. In case he could not give any satisfactory proof, his case would be referred to India for verification and that might take quite some time. He virtually started weeping. I offered him a glass of water. He told me in a pathetic voice that he loved his wife and he could no longer bear her separation. He added he was afraid of losing her because she was nor responding to so many letters that he had written to her. It was hard for me to make out if his tears were genuine, or as we say was he shedding crocodile tears to win my sympathy? Unfortunately he had no documentary proof of his marriage or any other document, such as letters exchanged. I declined to issue visa to him till his case was verified from India. I saw his sullen face. But at least in my presence or perhaps within the hearing distance of people in and around the Visa Office, he did not call me names or curse me.

I had another very interesting case. A woman in her forties came from Lahore to get a visa. In every visa application the applicant had to mention the places and the people he or she wanted to visit besides giving two references in India. Surprisingly she had omitted the name and address of the person she wanted to meet in India, though she did mention she wanted to visit Kanpur. The two referees given by her were Hindus, though she was a Muslim woman. I asked her to explain the omission and why she had given the names of the Hindus as referees. She gave me a strange story that sounded like the plot of some movie.

She said one of the referees was in fact her husband. When she was young she fell in love with him and secretly married him. But her parents dragged her to Pakistan. Nevertheless, her husband used to visit her every year and she visited him in Kanpur as often as she could. She had two sons from the marriage, both studying in Lahore; one in a Law College and the other in a Degree College. She told me with a sense of pride that both the sons were very intelligent and she felt proud of them. It so happened that for the last two years her husband, a lawyer by profession and strangely a member of Jan Sangh (a political party mainly consisting of conservative Hindus) had not visited her because he was refused visa by the Pakistan High Commission in New Delhi. She was anxious to see him. That was some time in the end of October, 1971 when for security reasons the grant of visa was restricted to the bare minimum. I told her politely that in the present circumstances I could not straightway issue a visa to her and asked her if she had any objection if I made a reference to India to get the facts, as mentioned by her in her application, verified. She replied with full confidence that she had the least objection because her husband was a prominent man in Kanpur and wielded great influence. I did make a reference to India but until I left Karachi no reply had come. Soon after the war broke out and our office in Karachi was closed. Obviously I do not know what happened to the case. Of course, I do not remember the name of the woman nor of her Hindu husband in Kanpur as alleged by her. When today I think of her courage to meet her Hindu husband despite opposition from her parents, I do admire the lady. But sometimes I have other thoughts. Was she telling the truth? I would have very much liked to see the report from India that, unfortunately, had not materalised before I left Pakistan.

I recall the case of a man who had two wives, one in India and one in Pakistan. Besides making best of both the worlds, he bought and sold merchandise somewhat like barter trade. It is quite possible his one wife did not know he had another, though a Muslim is entitled to four legal wives. When I asked him how he managed to keep both wives happy, he just smiled. He did not give me an explanation. I had my doubts if his was a genuine case. I referred the matter to India and until I left no reply had come. He never inquired again.

There were some tricksters too. A man had unbelievably twenty aliases. I do not know how he managed to get so many passports issued to him, all on different dates but from the same Passport Office. We recognized him from his photos and intelligence reports. When we challenged him, he denied he had passports in different names. He refused to disclose his real identity and we refused the visa to him. Quite likely he was refused visa in the first instance and he went on changing his name and passport to hoodwink us.

Once a man applied for a visa on the ground of death of his father in India. He did not attach any proof of his father's death. I called him for an interview and when I asked him if he had any document or a letter that could establish the identity of his father and his death, he took out a telegram from his pocket and showed it to me. The telegram had its origin in India but on looking closely I found the telegram was two years old. When I asked him why he had not visited his father just after his death, he could not give a satisfactory reply. On further questioning we found out he had managed to get the telegram from somebody in India, which was a common modus operandi those days.

It was not hard to understand how in sheer desperation or on the wrong advice of the touts hovering around the Visa Office, often the applicants would falsify the facts without weighing the consequences. Most of the applicants were undoubtedly poor and illiterate, and had half the family members in India and half in Pakistan. They had come to Pakistan with high hopes and felt frustrated when they could not make a reasonable living. I felt sorry for them, but I had my limitations. I had to work within the framework of rules and regulations, which I did not think, were that harsh as was often made out by critics and India bashers. Many Pakistanis overstayed in India either because of family compulsions or looking for employment opportunities or just did not want to return to Pakistan and thus disappeared in the localities thickly populated by the Muslims. It became difficult for the police to trace such people because of lack of any assistance and cooperation from the local Muslims. Quite a few were undesirable, men from the Pakistan intelligence wearing the masks of innocent visitors. In order to secure votes from the minority communities in India, the political party in power usually adopted lukewarm attitude in not taking stern measures against Pakistani Muslims who deliberately overstayed without any plausible cause.

Despite a large chunk of the economic and military aid from the United States of America there was absolutely no doubt that the lot of common man in Pakistan had not improved. Much of the economic aid went to the pockets of the top brass of Pakistan army, the bureaucrats and a few well-known politicians. Where Pakistan would have been, had not the United States of America for various political considerations and keeping in mind the geographical realities of South Asia and the cold war, liberally pumped in so much military and economic aid? In this respect Pakistan had been one of the luckiest countries. Emanating from strong religious ties and pungent sentiments of the Islamic brotherhood, some Muslim countries also from time to time came to the aid of Pakistan in her turbulent times. Their hands only made Pakistan so complacent that no leader ever deliberated to give a serious thought to self-reliance and self-sufficiency. Taking full advantage of the support and much backing of the United States of America and Muslim countries Pakistan chose to become a self-appointed champion of the cause of Muslims in the world. Since for historical reasons she was allergic to India, Pakistan had, right from her inception, indulged in Hate India campaign. But –

> Sheer numbers do not certainly a battle win
> Nor slogans and banners will a victory spin
>
> Playing religious cards may please bigots
> Fundamentalists may fire a thousand shots
>
> Discrimination in ranks but halts the march
> Poverty, disease and hunger a nation torch
>
> On loot and barbarity a people cannot thrive
> Pride of the past cannot make present survive
>
> Enmities will always a race trouble and tease
> Happiness comes with mutual respect and peace

There is no doubt that in pre-partitioned India both the Hindus and the Muslims have lived together, as good neighbours, as friends and even as relatives (some converted to Islam and some still remaining Hindus from the same family), but in spite of loud claims made by the believers in secularism, in majority of such cases the bonds were fragile and even questionable. Had it not been so, there would have no partition of India. Some of the historians blame the British for their policy of divide and rule, but there is no denying the fact that the seeds of discord were sown by the Muslim invaders who came to India from the north. The stories of their atrocities, mayhem and brutality must have been carried from one generation to another through word of mouth, folk tales and rural poetry. The wounds might have been healed, but the scars remained. These are the scars of history and even if we try to forget, the historians will never. Unfortunately, no two historians will agree on many basic issues. A historian, for instance, in Pakistan sees the history of India from Islamic viewpoint and similarly a historian from India will look at it from his viewpoint. The history books of one country rarely travel to the other country. Whatever a student reads in his school days and perhaps college days, it leaves indelible impressions on him that most likely and usually remains with him until his death. And how many people read history outside the academic circle? How many care to read history books written by the authors that belong to the country against whom he has through early inculcation of orthodox and conservative ideas and conditioning of mind, whether deliberately or through sheer ignorance, taken a rigid stand sometimes bordering on animosity and even insanity? The fault lies not so much with young minds but with the history books that are quite often twisted, distorted and misinterpreted in keeping with the ideology of the writer or that of his masters who pay him.

It is hard to imagine a society without any conflict or clash of interests. So long as the force of religion remains predominant, mutual mistrust and hatred will persist. We sometimes talk of putting moratorium on some burning issues of the day, but can we put a moratorium on religious activities that lead to fanaticism and fundamentalism and thus create fissures on our lovely and good earth? The day we agree to make religion a matter of personal faith confined to the four walls of the house, not spilled over to public places of worship, sanity and peace may return to us, if those were there before.

Chapter 1

The Making of Pakistan

Pakistan did not appear on the map of the world all of a sudden. Four entities have contributed to the creation of Pakistan. First comes God. He creates, destroys and recreates the world. He divides and subdivides at His will. Without Him nothing moves and works as the mankind in general believes. When and why He conceived the idea of dividing British India into India, that is Bharat, and Pakistan, only He knows and He will not share His secrets with man. History will consider the British, the Hindus and the Muslims responsible for the partition. History cannot blame God.

After God comes Prophet Mohammad. He laid the foundation of Islam. The Muslims say Mohammad was chosen by God to establish the religion of Islam. He might not have had Pakistan in his mind at that time, but he certainly wanted the entire world converted to Islam. He could not, in his lifetime, fulfill the dream of watching Islam spread over the universe but he did leave behind a number of staunch conservative followers who assiduously took upon themselves the sacred task of converting (quite often through violent and dubious means) the Christians, the Hindus, the Buddhists and all other creeds prevailing in the world, into Muslims. Had there been no Mohammad, there would not have been Islam and had there been no Islam, there would not have been Pakistan because Pakistan soon after her birth declared herself an Islamic state based on the shariat as enshrined in the Koran, the holy book of the Muslims.

The next entity is Mohammed Iqbal, also called Allama Iqbal. Incidentally, his first name is the same as that of Prophet Mohammed. In an acquisitive sense he conceived the idea of Pakistan by truncating undivided India. He was a highly educated man, a renowned poet of Urdu and Persian and a fiery propagator of Islam. He had studied at the Universities of Cambridge, Rome and Madrid. He travelled widely and met Mussolini, who as claimed by Muslim historians, had studied some of Iqbal's works (obviously translations) and familiarized himself with his philosophy. While Western education probably inculcated in him the spirit of freedom, Mussolini probably gave him the spirit to fight ruthlessly with weapons of words, scholarly ideas shaped into verses. Much of his poetry is emanated from the Islamic fundamentalism. He exhorted the Muslims, not only in India but wherever they were, to hoist the banner of Islam on the top of the world. He felt strongly that the Muslims everywhere had been treated shabbily (in India by the Hindus) and that was the cause of their poverty, ignorance and miserable neglect. He covertly preached revolt against the non-Muslim authority anywhere and everywhere it was. His poetry no doubt enthused and inspired many Muslims in India because they knew Urdu and Persian to a reasonable extent and could, therefore, read his original works. In the beginning of his political career he was secular-minded and advocated the unity of the Hindus and the Muslims, but later on he became an Islamic fundamentalist. In 1930 in his presidential address at the annual session of the Muslim League, for the first time, he brought in the concept of Pakistan where, as he visualized, the Muslims would live in full freedom, safe from the clutches of the Hindu banyas (traders) and the Hindu leaders, who as he thought, had no soft corner for the Muslims. He lost respect for Mahatma Gandhi even though Gandhi preached Hindu-Muslim unity and wanted all Indians irrespective of caste, creed and colour, to fight against the British as a coherent unit for the independence of

India. His disrespect for Gandhi perhaps arose from his misconceived belief that all Hindus were bad. All his life he had no Hindu friend.

Iqbal had some fanatical notions. He believed that the ancestors of Napoleon were of the Arabic origin and that the Arabs guided Vasco de Gama to India. While he exhorted the Muslims to strictly follow the tenets of Islam, paradoxically he himself dressed in western style – a suit with tie, though sometimes he did wear the cloak of a Muslim. While Islam enjoins a devout Muslim to shun the company of a non-Muslim, Iqbal hired a German governess to take care of his children – a boy and a girl - after the death of his wife. It was on her recommendation that he removed his daughter from a madrasa and sent her to a convent school where education was given in the English language and the Morning Prayer was based on the Bible. Incidentally, about two hundred years before his birth, his ancestors were the Hindus – the Kashmiri Brahmans. Not much is known why they converted themselves to Islam. Most probably they were converted with sword hanging over their heads as a substantial majority of people having diverse faiths were converted. Since the Kashmiri Brahmans were scholars, enjoyed high respect and were economically well off, except the fear of death at the hands of the Islamic jehadis (crusaders) any other reason for their conversion defies logic.

The last and not the least entity giving Pakistan a distinct place on the map of the world was Mohammed Ali Jinnah. By sheer coincidence his first name is the same as that of the prophet and Iqbal. He was born in Karachi on December 25, 1876. After matriculation he went to England to become a barrister. He started practicing at the High Court in Bombay at the age of tywentyone. After an initial failure, eventually he became a successful lawyer. He joined the All Indian Congress in 1906 but left it in 1920 after a resolution of non-cooperation with the British Government was passed. One theory is that unlike other Congressmen, he did not want to face bullets and rot in the jail. In fact, at that point of time he was the only Indian leader who never went to jail. While still in the Congress, he was attending the meetings of All India Muslim League that later on demanded a separate homeland for the Muslims. He became President of the League in 1940.

He was given to drinking. He was ignorant of the tenets of Islam. It seems he was not a fundamentalist but he was not willing to undergo sufferings. He found it convenient to advocate the cause of the Indian Muslims for a separate homeland. How the Muslims chose him as their leader, is an enigma. After he left Bombay where he used to practise law, he left his huge mansion behind. It is said when the Indian High Commissioner in Karachi told Jinnah that his house in Bombay would be taken over by the Government, he said to him, "Tell Jawaharlal (the then Prime Minister of India) not to break my heart. I have built it brick by brick...I look forward to going back there." But he never returned to India. He died on September 11, 1948, that is, thirteen months after he became Quaid-e-Azam, the Father of Nation (Pakistan). His secular ideas, despite pleading for the cause of Pakistan, did not find favour with the hardcore elements in the Muslim League including Liaqat Ali Khan, the first prime minister of Pakistan. Perhaps Jinnah regretted his decision in demanding Pakistan. Since he died sooner than expected, it is hard to know how his mind worked after the creation of Pakistan. Possibly he was a confused man – at least politically.

Like an individual, every nation has a quota of its luck in making and unmaking it. The British did not dislike Jinnah because unlike the leaders in the Congress he was the least vocal and provocative. The Muslims needed someone to lead and in him they found a ready answer. The political rift between the Congress and the British Government afforded him a golden opportunity to become the leader of the Muslims and they readily accepted him. The Muslims, it seems, had no alternative.

The first Prime Minister of India Jawaharlal Nehru was a socialist which to the good luck of Pakistan and the bad luck of

India was construed by capitalist society, in particular the United States of America, as a diluted version of communism. The little moral support that America gave to the movement for independence of India almost vanished when she found India drifting both politically and economically towards the Soviet Union. History has ample evidence to show that the USA and the USSR were sworn enemies. To counteract the influence and spread of communism the USA needed military bases in the Indian subcontinent and Pakistan came handy. From that time onwards Pakistan received both military and economic aid in abundance, which was indeed a blessing in disguise for her. The Lady Luck smiled on Pakistan. But for massive aid from the USA, Pakistan might have found it hard to survive. God came to the rescue of Pakistan in the guise of United States of America. The dictators in Pakistan, though copiously condemned by the American Press and derided by the White House and the State Department (more as a publicity stunt than in earnest), were easy to handle. It was convenient and less expensive to placate a few individuals in Pakistan than to help the millions of Indians who remained pledged to democracy. While India suffered at the hands of America, Pakistan thrived and unfortunately the Soviet Russia could not match to the USA in wealth and resources. What India received from the USSR was peanuts when compared to what Pakistan received from America.

To the consternation of India, the Soviet Union disintegrated, leaving her friendless, while to the good luck of Pakistan despite being a fertile ground for terrorists and making a mockery of democracy, America still has a fancy for her and has once again placed dictatorship on the high pedestal for her own ends. India knows well and perhaps some other countries know too that so long as Pakistan has the blessings of the United States of America amity between the two countries, that is India and Pakistan, is still a cherished dream. When that dream will transform into reality, is a million dollar question. Pakistan is a trusted friend and ally of the Americans, as alleged by many American leaders; the loyalty (blind faith) of India is yet to be tested. How long, only America knows.

Luck did not stop with America. There came China. In Pakistan, China found a common enemy in India. The border dispute between India and China was an exploded excuse for China to keep India struggling for survival so that India would never become a power to reckon with. Though China was no match to America in providing economic aid to Pakistan but providing nuclear technology whether directly or through North Korea, a communist ally, she saw to it that on the strength of her military prowess and striking power, Pakistan did not compromise with India. That is the game that has been played against India both by China and America though for different reasons.

India cannot close her eyes and the world cannot overlook the harsh reality that this unholy alliance (of course, holy to the parties) between China and Pakistan on the one side and between America and Pakistan on the other side – logistically a pincer movement in the war of nerves, has weakened India in the past and has forced her to spend billions of rupees on her defence, depriving a large majority of her citizens from leading a reasonable life free from poverty and want. The proclamations of good intentions towards India by China with the beat of a drum is a strategy well conceived and well executed to malign India in the eyes of the world and so long as America, the only superpower, conveniently ignores the mala fides of both China and Pakistan, India by her own efforts cannot convince the world that she is right and is on the right track.

Pakistan is an Islamic country, whereas India has a substantial majority of the Hindus. Islam is widely spread throughout the world, whereas Hinduism is basically confined to India and the tiny border state of Nepal. Through terrorists activities the fundamentalists in Islam have made their presence felt in non-Islamic countries, and Pakistan being a Muslim country fomenting trouble by training and abetting Islamic fundamentalists, in the background of clean chit given by the USA, has become conspicuous in the eyes of the non-Islamic countries, which are prone to listen to the loud protestations of Pakistan and believe in her repeated lies on Kashmir. Then Pakistan has the support of the Muslim countries and India stands isolated because there are no other countries populated by the Hindus. Here again Pakistan is lucky. In comparison, though a small country, Israel is able to keep the Muslim countries foaming in anger because the Jews have a strong lobby and a true friend in the USA. Everything in the world these days revolves round the USA. There was once a saying in the British Parliamentary system that the British Parliament could do anything except to turn a man into a woman and a woman into a man. The United States of America is a step ahead. It can do that too and like the old British Crown, the USA has ambitions too, perhaps wider and more questionable than England once had. India is obviously in a tight corner and to add to her woes the USA, despite being a democracy, likes to flirt with the dictators of Pakistan.

Lastly, next to Indonesia, India has the largest population of Muslims, more than what Pakistan has. Many Muslims of the older generation were in the forefront of the movement for the independence of India and fought equally with the Hindus against the British imperialism. They were definitely secular-minded and did not believe in two-nation theory, the trump card that Iqbal and Jinnah chose to demand a separate homeland for the Indian Muslims. While the majority of the Muslims in India are loyal to India, some Muslims, mostly the youth backed by a few hardcore mullahs funded by some of the Muslim countries including Pakistan, whether wholly or partially, ignorant of the history of India's independence and the sacrifices their fathers made to achieve that goal, have been purposively misguided in the name of Islam to wage a holy war against the infidels that besides India ironically includes the USA too, as a sacred duty towards Allah. The lure of easy money and a spirit of adventure like old time British hunters in India with guns in their hands hounding for tigers and elephants have complicated the situation. To track down those fundamentalists in India is a Herculean task and since they cannot be eliminated or stopped from the old Naga practice of head hunting, encouraged, aided and abetted across the border by Pakistan, they pose an internal danger to the security and freedom of India. It may be easier to fight an external enemy, but it is almost impossible to fight an internal enemy when you don't know who in the crowd your friend is and who the enemy?

Even if the Kashmir issue is resolved, though it seems doubtful in the present circumstances, to the satisfaction of both the parties, the possibility of amity and friendship between the two countries is a pious dream that only God can fulfill. And when God will desire it, we cannot say. The Pakistani military rulers, who have in aggregate ruled longer than the civilian governments, have time and again called Kashmir a core issue between the two countries. Apparently it appears so to the wandering eyes, but in reality the core issue is Islamic fundamentalism. No Pakistani ruler, even a civilian, can afford to detach himself from the mullahs and the maulvis (heads of religious institutions including mosques and madrasas) in Pakistan, and unfortunately religion is the only weapon available to the Pakistani rulers to keep the poor masses happy and content (that is the will of God), and keep the same masses in good humor, India comes handy to Pakistan. No leader has the will and guts to declare religion a personal affair and offer India a hand of friendship on secular basis. The India pot has to be kept boiling. It fetches military and economic aid from the USA on the plea that balance of power has to be maintained in the subcontinent to the joy and satisfaction of the USA. India's alliance with the erstwhile Soviet Union is still fresh in the mind of the State Department, the think-tank of the US foreign policy. No President of the USA, howsoever open-minded, broadminded and a man of independent thinking, can completely ignore the advice of the State Department, and the fact remains, Presidents will come and go, but the records and archives of the State

Department will remain, if not for ever, for many decades. No nation conveniently forgets its history, particularly when it has not been to its taste.

Despite the presence of a large number of well wishers on both sides of the border between India and Pakistan and exchange of diverse groups from different walks of life, a lasting peace is a far cry. While India has lived by dint of her own efforts, Pakistan has been pampered and bottle-fed right from her birth both by the USA and China and some Muslims countries, whatever the reasons may be. She hates to work and if there is peace on both sides, the leaders of Pakistan will have to forgo their comforts that they will never like to lose. Pakistan is a convenient tool in the hands of the USA and China that they will not like to loosen. It is not a prediction. It is not pessimism. It is a ground reality that we can see with our naked eyes.

But the problem is not insoluble. A lasting and durable peace is possible if the two countries become one again, either by opening their boarders with least travel restrictions or more logically by forming a sort of confederation. Religious bigotry is not a newly born babe. It was there in the past and it will be there in future. If man can live in spite of droughts, famines, floods, typhoons, earthquakes, deadly diseases, wars and poverty, he can also live with the religious bigotry of a few. It needs will power. Who will bell the cat? That is, of course, a big question. Because of long history of mistrust right from the time of the partition, India may be as hesitant to take a step forward as Pakistan may be. Since the mistrust on either side is not all ill-founded, rebuilding the trust needs the goodwill of countries like the USA and China. How far these two countries will go to bring India and Pakistan together is a difficult preposition because both have vested interest in Pakistan. Unfortunately, as there is not much love between the USA and China, any expectation of a coordinated approach from them is a pious dream. Only time will mend the broken bones.

Chapter 2

Bangladesh

Just as there was marriage of convenience between Pakistan and the United States of America on the one hand and between Pakistan and China on the other, despite different ideologies, with the avowed object of forming a common front against India though for different reasons, there was the same sort of marriage of convenience between West Pakistan and East Pakistan despite different cultures with the avowed object of forming a common front against the Hindus in India. Islam was the only link that bound the West with the East of Pakistan that, of course, did not stand the test of time. The myth exploded as soon as Mujib-ur-Rahman declared independence from West Pakistan and gave East Pakistan the name of Bangladesh. There were economic, cultural and lingual differences between the two wings besides a distance of more than a thousand miles through the Indian territory. Let us see those differences first.

1. **Language and Culture.** While in the four provinces of Pakistan Urdu was more or less commonly understood though in the Punjab that constituted 65% of the population of West Pakistan people spoke Punjabi, in Sind the Sindhi, in NWFP the Pushto and in Baluchistan the Baluchi, in East Pakistan the people spoke Bengali. The Bengalis had absolutely no knowledge of Urdu and whatever little

Urdu they knew or spoke that was inducted by the West Pakistanis – the business community, the professionals and the Government servants transferred from West Pakistan. While the Bengalis did make some effort to learn Urdu, the West Pakistan rather shunned Bengali. It would not be incorrect to say that they almost hated Bengali language because they believed it was the language of Hindu banyas (traders). The Government of Pakistan gave no encouragement to the Bengali language; rather she tried to erode it from the soil of East Pakistan by inducting Urdu in the schools. That was one of the traumatic experiences gone through by the Bengalis, a majority of whom despite lack of education and poverty loved their language and their culture. Imposition of Urdu was not less than a cultural genocide of the Bengali language. Both the Hindus and the Muslims in undivided Bengal shared and enjoyed Bengali literature, whether it came from a Hindu writer or a Muslim writer it did not matter. The heritage of rich Bengali culture gave them a sense of pride and perhaps some superiority complex too. Nobody, not even for academic sake, in West Pakistan was interested in the Bengali literature. No ostensible effort was made to translate the Bengali literature into Urdu. The Government of Pakistan dominated by the West Pakistanis, mostly the Punjabis, was least interested to introduce the Bengali literature in the curricula of the schools and the colleges. How could they be interested when their object was to erase Bengali from the soil of East Pakistan perhaps in the same manner the early converts to Islam tried to destroy and denigrate the language, the old culture and civilization of the natives in India and elsewhere. In their view the Bengalis in East Pakistan were like infidels who needed conversion to true Islam as envisaged and propagated by the mullahs and maulvis in West Pakistan with the support of the politicians and the Government of Pakistan, sometimes overtly and other times covertly.

The Muslims of West Pakistan more steeped in the Islamic Ideology of the last Mughal Emperor Aurangzeb had absolutely no taste for classical music, dance and drama and other fine arts like sculpture and painting in sharp contrast to the Bengalis who loved various forms of art and literature. The taste of the West Pakistanis was limited to mujras (dancing and singing girls), mirasis (drum beaters) and mushairas (assembly of Urdu poets). There were, of course, some good singers of gazals both among men and women, but none who had a nick in the classical music. There were no academies or institutions for giving instructions in music, dance and drama. Governed by rigid Islamic code, there were no learners either. All the literature was in local languages, mostly Punjabi and Sindhi, limited to fiction, short stories, novels, and poetry. There were hardly any intellectuals and thinkers in West Pakistan.

2. **Colour of Skin and Features.** While the people of West Pakistan had a fair complexion, the Bengalis in East Pakistan had a dark complexion. Of course, there were many exceptions but basic colour contrasts did exist. The West Pakistanis especially the Punjabis had a great fancy for white skin (that even the Hindus and the Sikhs had before they migrated to India) not paying the same kind of attention to features. The Bengalis, on the contrary, had good features. Their women, in particular, had curvaceous bodies, deep-set eyes and long dark shiny hair that almost reached the waistline. On the contrary the women of West Pakistan were usually fluffy, heavy and with irregular formation of body lines. Whereas the women and men of Bengal had some sort of refinement in their manners and presentation, the men and women of West Pakistan were usually rough, rude and uneducated.

Those men and even some women also made a liberal use of vulgar and indecent language in daily conversation though nobody minded it. That might have some thing to do with lack of education and unsettled conditions caused by the repeated incursions by the invaders from the North. Though some West Pakistanis did marry the Bengali women, they did not like their cooking and manner of beautifying themselves. Since a Muslim could have four wives, many West Pakistanis, particularly the business community having establishments in both the wings, had at least one wife in Karachi or Lahore and one in Dacca or Chittagong. Well-versed in the technique of allurement, the Pakistani men from the West Wing taking full advantage of the poverty of the Bengali region in general, found it easy to lure the Bengali women into their harem. Quite a few used the Bengali women back in West Pakistan for menial jobs and for prostitution in the same way the Arabs from the Gulf countries did when they took young girls as wives from the poor Muslim families in India on payment of handsome money to their parents with the promise of sending more in future. Flesh trade has no religion and no morals as it has no colour and age considerations. The Muslims from West Pakistan were equally deficient in appreciating the screen beauty of the Bengali actresses. Other that the black hair and the blackberries, the West Pakistani had a sort of aversion to the black colour, particularly of the skin. Just as the Britishers called a native Indian 'kala admi' (black man), the West Pakistanis called a Bengali 'kala tawa' (black iron plate used in making chapattis). This sort of colour prejudice did annoy the Bengalis.

3. **Commerce and Industry:** There was no worthwhile industry, not even on small scale, in either wing of Pakistan and for that matter, in fact, there was no industry worth the name in the whole of undivided India. The British

Government for her own selfish ends laid great emphasis on the development of agriculture because England being a small country could not feed a big country of the size of India, but she could conveniently and profitably supply goods manufactured in English factories or procured from the countries of Europe, the partners in progress and prosperity. Both the Wings of Pakistan exported limited raw materials available. While the West exported textiles, leather, wheat, carpets and some sports goods, the East exported raw jute and jute products, seafood, rice, tea and sugarcane. But the foreign exchange earned by the East Wing was much more than that earned by the West Wing. Unfortunately for the East Pakistan, almost 75 to 80% of the foreign exchange earned was spent on development in West Pakistan and on import of luxury goods by the rich in West Pakistan that besides the business community included either the politicians in power or the military brass and the high bureaucrats, who had gradually become rich through corrupt practices in collusion with the politicians and the military clan. Not only that, whatever economic and military aid, Pakistan got from the USA, a major chunk of it went to the share of the West Pakistanis. The Government of Pakistan might have manoeuvred statistics to present a fair picture of distribution of wealth in both the Wings, but how long could they throw dust into the eyes of the Bengalis?

There was another economic disparity that caused more inflation in East Pakistan than in West Pakistan. As the Government of Pakistan was not interested in developing industry in East Pakistan, many manufactured items like textiles including made-ups, leather goods and shoes, cooking oils and cooking pots and salt came all the way from West Pakistan after traversing a distance of more than a thousand miles by sea, adding to the landed cost besides the indiscriminate profiteering by the suppliers. It was like the old British policy of importing raw materials from India and sending manufactured goods back to India from England. The Bengalis naturally suffered economically at the hands of their brethren in West Pakistan, who had taken East Pakistan for granted as a fertile area for exploitation and economic dominance. Nobody in West Pakistan perhaps ever thought that one day not in too distant future East Pakistan could slip away from their hold, howsoever tight.

4 **Exploitation of Manpower:** Other than economic, cultural and sexual exploitation, the West Pakistanis equally exploited the surplus manpower in East Pakistan to their full advantage. They took the poor Bengalis to work in the factories in West Pakistan at lesser wages than they paid to their counterparts from West Pakistan and deprived them of many benefits like medical assistance, housing and insurance against accident and death. Separated from their families by hundreds of miles, those poor people had no money to go home on vacation or leave and because of limited means could not either call their families to join them. Many were employed as domestic help with the minimum wages or practically no wages other than a small place to live, food to eat and discarded clothes to wear. There was no Government Department to listen to them; forget ventilating their grievances. They could be fired any time without assigning any reason. No compensation was paid, and some were left on the road to beg.

Among all the communities in British India the Muslims were the least educated or at the most they went to the madrasas where the emphasis was on the teachings of the Koran rather than on subjects like Science, Mathematics, Economics and History. Their world revolved round the holy place of Mecca that was a source of inspiration and motivation for spreading Islam throughout the world than discovering the world through learning and research in cooperation with other nations. Literally speaking they remained confined to their religious dreams and relied too much on the will of God. When the British opened schools in India imparting modern education, a substantial majority of Muslims shunned the very idea of enrolling their children. The reins of the British Administration in India were in the hands of the Englishmen, who occupied high positions and after them the educated Hindus and a few educated Muslims stepped in. The situation was practically the same in the armed forces. With the partition of British India there was, therefore, a sudden vacuum in the civil services and armed forces of Pakistan which was filled through speedy recruitment that temporarily helped the Government in reducing the unemployment. Once again, to the consternation of the Bengalis, a majority of new recruits, especially in the armed forces were from West Pakistan. That caused much heart burning among the Bengalis. Besides, many high posts in East Pakistan were taken over by the officers from the West Pakistan. Even teachers were sent to East Pakistan from West Pakistan. In nutshell, the West Pakistan dominated the East Pakistan in every conceivable sphere.

5. **Dress and Food:** The manner in which the men and women of West Pakistan especially the women dressed themselves was completely different from that of the Bengalis. The women of West Pakistan either wore salwar (baggy type pajamas) and kamiz (loose shirt) or ghagra (kind of loose flowing skirt) and used burqa (covering the entire body) though confined to the middle urban class, the Bengali women wore sari and did not use burqa. The poor Muslim women that formed bulk of the female population in West Pakistan, could not afford a burqa that required anywhere from five to six yards of cloth besides

tailoring charges that they could not afford. Though most of the Bengali women were also poor, they used saris of lesser length than the usual six yards of cloth. Sari was virtually a taboo in West Pakistan and looked down upon by the Muslim Community because it was associated with the Hindus.

Most of the men in the urban areas of West Pakistan also wore salwar and kamiz, though stitched slightly different from that of the women and less colourful and ostentatious. They covered their heads with turbans, some quite stylish. The village folk wore tahmat or dhoti (a piece of unstitched buttonless cloth worn round the loins), usually made of white coarse cloth and a short kamiz. In winter, which was quire severe in many parts, the city dwellers used cotton-filled parkas or shawls, while the country folk covered their bodies with thick sheets or razais (cotton blankets) that they also used at night when sleeping. Since the Bengalis did not have to face the rigours of a harsh winter, their dress remained the same throughout the year. The men also wore dhotis but usually made from coloured striped cloth. The West Pakistanis used jootis (open shoe without laces made from leather), the Bengalis used slippers. The people in high positions and the rich class also put on Western style shoes, whose price was beyond the reach of the common man.

While the staple food of the West Pakistanis was wheat and goat meat, the Bengalis ate rice and fish. The West Pakistanis made rotis (round shaped bread either baked in a tandoor (a clay oven) or on an iron plate called tawa), paranthas (rotis stuffed with vegetables like cauliflower, potatoes, etc or minced meat) and nans from atta (wheat flour). They also used coarse grains like bajra, maize, and the like. West Pakistan did grow rice, usually of inferior quality used for making khichri (rice

> cooked with lentils). The superior quality rice like Basmati was used in preparing biryani (rice cooked with meat) or pilaf (sweet rice with a liberal use of dry fruit), which were a sort of delicacy rather a regular menu. The Bengalis had virtually no idea of making dishes from wheat. For cooking in West Pakistan people used pure ghee or hydrogenated oil, in East Pakistan mustard oil was commonly consumed besides grooming the hair. The West Pakistanis had little taste for fish though in winter there was some consumption mostly by the upper class. While in West Pakistan sweets were mainly made from besan (gram flour) and maida (fine wheat flour), in East Pakistan the best sweets were prepared from milk. Incidentally, the khansamas (cooks) in West Pakistan were no match to the Bengali chefs, some of whom were well renowned. The food habits of the people in the two Wings were as dissimilar as their culture and language.

Perturbed by gross injustice and discrimination at the hands of the West Pakistanis, the escalating grouses and legitimate grievances of the Bengalis gravitated to a demand for complete independence from Pakistan perhaps in the same manner when fanned by the wind of religious bigotry the Muslims in undivided India demanded a separate homeland for the Muslims free from the alleged dominance of the Hindu community. It is a different matter that unlike the grievances of the Bengalis, the grievances of the Muslims against the Hindus were grossly unfounded. The Muslims did not realize that the root cause of their poverty coupled with lack of employment opportunities was because of their gross deficiency in modern education. The Muslims were reluctantly slow in learning English language and pathetically dull in Mathematics and Science subjects. Contrary to the West Pakistanis, the Bengalis despite large scale poverty were not averse to learning their own language and the modern subjects, though unfortunately again because of wide-spread poverty their schooling was limited.

Complete dissatisfaction with the Central Government dominated by the West Pakistanis over life and death matters of language, trade and commerce and employment besides cultural antagonism angered the Bengalis, who luckily found a leader of great caliber in Sheikh Mujib-ur-Rahman, the soul of Awami League, the main political party of East Pakistan. A determined and dedicated man as Mujib was, he raised his voice against the autocratic rule of the West Pakistan that both the political and the military rulers justified in the name of Islam. When the West Pakistan turned a deaf ear to the genuine demands of the Bengalis, Mujib became their chief spokesman. He now demanded full autonomy for the Bengalis. The Government of Pakistan jailed him twice in 1960 and in 1966. Under fear of popular discontentment among the Bengalis that had all the ingredients of a revolution, he was freed in 1969. But the cyclonic surge of the freedom movement that had already sent alarming signals to Islamabad was hard to contain. A huge cyclone in 1970 that almost devastated the coastal regions of East Bengal added fury to the political cyclone when the West Pakistanis from all sections of the society did practically nothing to help the poor people trampled and torn by the tempestuous waves that demolished houses and huts, uprooted trees and caused floods. The response of the Government of Pakistan was miserably poor. The anger of Bengalis now acquired the dimensions of a cyclone. Irrespective of their political affiliations and religious links, the Bengalis stood united as a single entity, ready to make sacrifices of any kind to achieve the goal of total detachment from their so-called brethrens in West Pakistan.

The misery of the Bengalis was compounded when the West Pakistan blatantly refused to install Mujib as the next Prime Minister of Pakistan after his Awami League party had swept the polls getting a clear majority. The Bengalis were left with no doubt in their minds that nothing would come out of their remaining a part and parcel of Pakistan. When under the command of Mujib their demand for liberation grew vociferous and volatile, Yaha Khan, the President and the Martial law Administrator of Pakistan ordered his men to arrest Mujib. On the night of March 25, '71 Mujib was whisked away from his residence in Dhan Mandi and taken surreptitiously to West Pakistan. Fearing an uprising in East Pakistan, Yahya Khan launched Operation Searchlight, a ruthless and sustained assault on the Bengalis with the clear object of subjugating them to the end. No correct figure of the Bengalis massacred by the Military men of Pakistan under orders from Yahya Khan is available, but the observes all over the world put the figure anywhere between two to three million. Over and above, about ten million Bengalis including a large number of the Hindus fled to take refuge in neighbouring India. That was a big problem for India, especially for the West Bengal where the Bengalis from East Pakistan found a safe haven from the atrocities and mayhem of the West Pakistani soldiers.

Most of the leaders of Awami League were successful in escaping to India. They wasted no time in setting up a Government-in-Exile of Bangladesh in Calcutta. The Government of India was in a precarious situation. Pakistan had the overt or covert support of both the USA and China, who were threatening India with dire consequences if she meddled in the internal affairs of Pakistan. Though India had the full backing of the erstwhile USSR, but she could not ignore the threats posed by the USA and China. Under the leadership of Indira Gandhi, the then Prime Minister of India, bold steps were taken by India to help Bengali guerrilla force called Mukti Bahini to fight against the Pakistani armed forces. Had India not given moral and material support besides logistic guidance, the task of Mukti Bahini to liberate East Pakistan would have been very difficult, could be even unachievable. India had no choice. Much of the world under the influence of the USA and European countries, mainly the England, almost turned a deaf ear when India vehemently vocalized the voice of aggrieved and ambushed Bengalis. Besides, no nation of the world, not even the UNO dominated by the USA, gave any tangible assistance and aid to the millions of the Bengali refugees in India. Whatever aid came, that was both too low and too slow.

The writing was on the wall. Yahya Khan and his proteges did not read it or if they read it, they closed their eyes like the proverbial parrot closing his eyes on seeing a cat that the danger was over. Frustrated and baffled, unable to think rationally, without weighing the consequences, Yahya Khan ordered his army to attack Kashmir thinking that either India would withdraw her forces from the borders with East Pakistan to protect Kashmir making his task of subjugating the Bengalis easier or withdraw some of her forces from Kashmir to concentrate on East Pakistan. He calculated either way Pakistan would be the gainer. In fact, the gamble was mainly for Kashmir. The gamble failed. India won the war of 1971. Ninety thousand prisoners of war were taken by India. The end of Indo-Pakistan war gave birth to Bangladesh.

Chapter 3

Seven Months in Pakistan — 1971

April 14

I saw more Pathans and Punjabis than Sindhis. The Punjabi and Pashto-speaking people seemed to have penetrated Karachi. Urdu is understood and spoken fairly well. However, the signboards are mostly in English. Men generally wear salwar (white or light coloured) and kamiz that goes below the knees. Most of the women are in burqa.

April 15

Sadar, a big shopping center in Karachi has all types of shops full of goods of which a substantial quantity like packed food items, toilet goods, cosmetics, electrical gadgets, clothes, shoes etc. is imported. While going through the market and looking at the labels one finds that Pakistan's own contribution to the manufactured articles of daily use seems insignificant when compared with India. However, almost all types of fruits and fresh vegetables in season, produced in Pakistan, are available at moderate prices barring a few. Essential items like lemons, supari (betel nuts), tea, coffee and certain spices, which are either imported or come from East Pakistan, are rather expensive. There is, otherwise, no dearth of items of daily use. One redeeming feature of the market condition is that for fear of being punished by the military jaunta, the shopkeepers dare not overcharge or sell anything in black market, though, as I learnt from my colleague, there are instances of giving short measures. It is difficult to detect the shortness because the scales and weights used by the shopkeepers are still of the old type.

English daily newspapers like DAWN and MORNING NEWS use a very poor quality of paper and the coverage is even worse. Of eight pages, almost two pages cover cinema advertisements and four are devoted to vicious propaganda against India. Pakistani press is a past master in fabrication. The horrifying and sensational accounts of Indian armed forces infiltration into East Pakistan are fantastic. They read like fairy tales. It seems the proprietors of these papers bound by censor rules and instigated by the Government have to concoct some stories to fill the pages of the newspaper.

Unlike in India Pakistan does not have a vibrant film industry. Most of the films are imported from USA and are either very old or cheap stuff like mystery thrillers or cowboy stories that one can easily make out from the advertisements in the newspapers. Screening of films from India is banned. In fact, anything from India is a taboo.

April 16

I do not feel like reading the Pakistani newspapers in the morning that are full of mud-slinging and malicious propaganda against India. It is so disgusting. Whether an average Pakistani is carried away by this type of press hysteria fully backed and instigated by the Military regime is hard to say. But when a lie is repeatedly told it eventually comes nearer to be accepted as a truth. Today's newspapers carried a photograph of a huge procession shouting anti-Indian slogans and carrying anti-Indian banners parading the streets of Dacca to protest against the infiltration of Indian armed forces into East Pakistan. Strangely, nothing could be deciphered from the banners and placards. It looked as if blots of ink had been spread on the cloth and the papers to look like words. When nothing could be read, the purpose of the procession was unclear unless one strictly went by the newspaper caption. Who would certify the genuineness of the photograph when there is no correspondent from East Pakistan stationed in West Pakistan. It could be some old clipping from a stale newspaper, perhaps the Bengalis protesting against their own Government.

To cover up her own record of atrocities and ruthless killings in East Pakistan, Pakistan is deliberately and mischievously implicating India for creating chaotic conditions in the Eastern part. How far anti-India tirade has an appeal to the masses is hard to say. A common man, as it strikes to me, wants to live in peace. He is more worried about his daily bread (forget the butter) than politics. What I can sense is that people in general have lost faith in the leadership of Pakistan after the 1965 conflict with India. I gather from a source that after the hijacking of the Indian Airline plane, some students took out a procession to demonstrate in front of Indian High Commission. On their way the students stoned every building owned or occupied by any foreign organization. They looted some shops owned by their Muslim brethren. As soon as the police were called in, the procession dispersed. The marchers never reached the Indian High Commission building. From that day on Section 144 (banning assembly of five or more persons in public places) is still in force.

Our Bengali Muslim domestic servant tells us that soon after the military action in East Pakistan, 200 to 300 Bengalis in Karachi alone were killed by the fanatics. The people of West Pakistan mostly the Punjabis who constitute 65% of the population of West Pakistan, consider Mujib-ur-Rahman, the acknowledged leader of the Bengalis in East Pakistan, a sworn enemy of Pakistan.

Not only the Pakistani press but also Pakistan radio, which is controlled by the Government, is full of vitriolic and virulent propaganda against India. The songs and plays broadcast every day through dirty caricatures, filthy satire and abusive language, make a mockery of Indian leaders and merchant class calling them bloodsuckers while branding India as their bitter enemy.

April 17

The people we meet in daily life have apparently no hostile attitude towards us, but they do not like to mix with us for fear of being harassed by men from the Pakistan intelligence service present in large number in plain clothes outside the High Commission building and our residences. They follow us wherever and whenever we go out of our homes. It is not safe to go alone to any place or have even a stroll after an evening meal. Our people always carry their identity cards or passports with them as and when they step out of their houses. The police have no scruples. Their whole object is to harass us, as far and as much possible.

Though we are allowed to import articles of daily use, the Government of Pakistan takes unusually long time to grant Exemption Certificate and postal authorities never send intimation to us about any article that has been ordered by us through mail order, leaving aside delivering it at our doorsteps (a postman's duty). Local people like masons, electricians and carpenters are reluctant to enter our buildings for repairs for fear of being questioned by the Pakistan Intelligence. Since such people are illiterate, they can be easily harassed by the Pakistan CID who perhaps expects them to bring some information from us that might be useful to them and when they have nothing to tell, the CID suspects them of concealment and hence, gets rough and tough with them.

April 18

The hoisting of the Bangladesh flag on the building of Pakistan High Commission in Calcutta mostly manned by the Bengalis from East Pakistan, as broadcast by the BBC and AIR in their evening bulletins, would definitely add a new dimension to the deteriorating relations between the two countries. The reaction of the Government of Pakistan may come any time. Pakistan may ask India to eject Mr. Hasan Ali, the Deputy High Commissioner (DHC) and consequently appoint a new DHC or Pakistan may quietly ask India to close her Mission in Dacca and projecting it as a retaliatory measure prompted by India's action, may close her Mission in Calcutta and thus recall her personnel to Pakistan, though such people returning to Pakistan seems most unlikely, where they would definitely face the charges of rebellion against their own Government and ultimately face the gallows.

Pakistan Radio today equated India with Israel and called for a summit conference of the Muslim countries to coordinate measures both against India and Israel. Pakistan knows well that playing the Israel card will invoke the sympathy of the Muslim countries.

In the background of the hoisting of Bangladesh flag, Pakistan's claim of return of normalcy in East Pakistan (East Bengal) reads like a farce. It is anybody's guess how long Pakistan can mislead the world and throw dust into the eyes of her own people.

April 20

The reaction of the Government of Pakistan to the hoisting of Bangladesh flag on the building of Pakistan's Deputy High Commission in Calcutta may come any time. The delay in the reaction indicates some confusion and panic in the mind of military dictatorship.

Vulgarity is the chief characteristic and main tone of Pakistan Press and more so of Pakistan Radio. Cheap satirical exposition in low taste bordering on hysteria is the hallmark of Pakistani propaganda against India.

In Pakistan people are either very rich or very poor. Of course, the rich can be counted on fingers. They are happy with the anti-India stance of the Government as it keeps the bureaucracy occupied with their own problems leaving them free to exploit the poor and labour class. Zulfkar Ali Bhutto himself is a rich man, possibly possessing 200 to 300 acres of fertile land. If he could get a majority for his party and thus muster so much power, it was solely due to the financial backing of the aristocracy, who want to protect their wealth and safeguard their interests at all costs. It is so easy to buy the votes of the poor.

The poor do not have the desire and courage to raise any voice against the Government or clamour for democratic rights for two potent reasons. First of all they are more concerned and worried about their daily bread than with the country's politics. Secondly, they are mortally afraid of the bullets from the military regime. Though unlike Hindus the Muslims are not fatalistic, they do have a blind faith in the will of God. They attribute their poverty to God's will than to the misdeeds of their leaders.

Shops are full with all sorts of goods but it appears people do not have much purchasing power. Crowds at shops or buying sprees are virtually unknown.

AIR News Bulletin of 9 PM (8.30 P.M. Pakistan Standard Time) airs the news that the Government of Pakistan has designated a new DHC for Calcutta. Strangely, neither the Pakistan Radio nor the Press has so far carried the story. The Government does not want to give even an inkling of the happenings in East Pakistan to her people in the West. Broadcasting the news of the hoisting of Bangladesh flag on the building of Pakistan Commission in Calcutta and thus suddenly appointing a new DHC would have definitely led to all sorts of speculations and rumours and street talk.

At this stage Pakistan does not seem to be interested in breaking diplomatic relations with India or winding up their Mission in Calcutta. Perhaps she thinks by keeping the Calcutta Mission working, she will have first hand knowledge of the events in neighbouring West Bengal connected with the desertion of Bengali staff and India's stand on declaration of independent Bangladesh.

April 21

The newspapers, whether in English or in Urdu, devote very little space to economic development because, as it seems, there is very little economic activity at present. Entire trade and industry is in the hands of a few rich people. The story goes that the trade and industry of the entire Pakistan is controlled by twenty odd families. They are least bothered about the lot of the common man.

Pakistan's main energies are directed against India. HATE INDIA seems to be their goal and perhaps life ambition. Even top ranking journalists indulge in the game of maligning India. The following paragraph from one Aziz Beg's "Pakistan Faces India" will illustrate the point: -

"There is such a grave gap between India's promises and performances that her leaders seem to be afflicted with schizophrenia. Pathologically speaking, it is a case of morbid behavior fit for clinical examination. All prescriptions are rejected because the patient is allergic to anatomy and refuses to listen and look at the writing on the wall. Will anything work? There is no talismanic formula, but time is a relentless teacher. How long can Indian rulers sit back with cotton stuffed in their ears? They shall have to accept the verdict of the people tomorrow, even if the court has adjourned today. But can they really afford the luxury of getting wiser after the event? There is enough fire to make the Kashmir cauldron boil over again. They will have to pay an exorbitant interest on this deferred political payment".

HATE INDIA campaign has acquired a notoriety. The competition is who can throw more mud and hurl abuses at India. The entire Government machinery is occupied with the theme of insinuating and maligning India. Both cultural and economic activities seem to have receded into the background. The propaganda machinery in Pakistan is running three shifts a day producing venom for India. In my entire life I have never seen one country using offensively abusive language against another.

I shudder at the very thought of mentioning the derisive and derogatory language employed both by the Pakistan Press and the Pakistan Radio.

April 23

Every failure in Pakistan is attributed to India. Every calamity in Pakistan is attributed to India. Every internal trouble in Pakistan is attributed to India. If there is illiteracy in Pakistan, it is because of Hindu influence before partition or Hindu teachers (as in East Bengal). If there are heavy rains, it is because India triggered artificial clouds. If the departure of Pakistan's cricket team has been delayed for 48 hours it is because of mischief caused by India. If the crops fail it is because the water in the river Jehlum coming from Indian Kashmir is without energy sucked by the electric power generated by India.

Even the intelligentsia in Pakistan is suffering from Indiaphobia, which is being systematically injected into the minds of the younger generation. If this trend continues, the relationship between India and Pakistan will be analogous to that between Israel and the Arab States. The chances of any reconciliation between the two countries seem very dim as Pakistan's anti-India stance has virtually reached a point of no return. Any retrogressive step by any leader in Pakistan would be suicidal for him. He would be accused by all and sundry of being bought by the enemy. Nobody in Pakistan would like to commit that kind of harakiri.

Pakistan's friendship with China is one of expediency as otherwise Islamic tenets and teachings run contrary to Communist ideology. Knowing Pakistan's rather inborn hostility towards India, China is fully exploiting the situation to her advantage.

April 24

We are not sure what is likely to happen to our Mission. It may be closed down or its strength reduced. We live in a state of suspense because we cannot by any stretch of imagination predict even immediate future.

Ever since I came here I have not been able to plan anything. Can I bring my family from India and if so, when? Can I visit Muzaffargarh, my birthplace? Can I cultivate local people and strike some friendship? I don't seem to have the answer to any of these questions.

Karachi is hot and humid. But evenings are usually pleasant and cool.

April 25

The cracks in Pakistan's economy are coming to the surface. The January-June import policy has been thoroughly revised and imports of many items drastically cut. A press release issued by the Government of Pakistan says that the dislocation of trade and industry during recent weeks has resulted in pressure on the balance of payments position. This has necessitated changes in import policy.

The media at the behest of the Government is adopting a threatening posture towards India as is clear from the concluding part of the editorial in today's *Dawn*:

"After such brutal exposure of her crimes (interference in the internal affairs of Pakistan, Farakha issue, Luxmipur occupation, Berubari betrayal, Batngarh butchery), the only honourable and practical alternative for India now is to retrace her steps and to make amends by stopping interference in the affairs of her neighbours. Her refusal to do so, even now, may have grave repercussions at a time and place that may not at all be palatable to her." That is the language that usually China speaks against India and Taiwan. Obviously, Pakistan has the patting and pressure of China.

Judging from the present mood of the bureaucrats and the business magnates East Bengal (if West Pakistan can manage to hold it) will finally be a colony of slaves. Any West Pakistani, who can afford and manage such a luxury, will love to have at least one wife in West Pakistan and one in East Pakistan (by

Muslim law he is entitled to have four wives); a cook and domestic servants from East Pakistan because Bengalis, presumably partly because of abject poverty and partly because of lack of employment opportunities in East Pakistan, are docile and submissive in sharp contrast to their counterparts from other provinces of Pakistan. An affluent Punjabi or a Sindhi will think ten times before employing a Pathan or a Baluchi as his servant or a chauffeur.

April 26

The daily claim made by Pakistani media that normalcy has returned to East Pakistan is a blatant lie. If it so, why the foreign correspondents are being refused accreditation?

The manner in which India is maligned by Pakistan media for her ills – economic, political, social and educational—has left no scope for rapprochement between the two countries. A break off in diplomatic relations between India and Pakistan seems inevitable. But when, that is hard to say at this moment.

The liberal policy of India in granting visas to Pakistani nationals has not paid any dividends. In a country where the common man has no voice, his genuine and well-intentioned desire to see amity and good neighbourly relations between the two countries has no value. He is, in fact, least bothered by the anti-India propaganda leashed by the Government of Pakistan.

There is complete censorship of news, but there is no censorship on abuses hurled at India. Perhaps this is the only way a writer or a journalist can get his write-up or an article published in a newspaper and thus make a living. All the abuses listed in any dictionary seem to have been exhausted. The writer looks for the new imprecations and name callings in local dialects, particularly from Punjabi and Multani that abound in filthy and indecent jokes making banal and brazen use of the sexual organs of both men and women.

April 27

A new theory is being advanced by the Pakistan media of equating India with Israel in order to whip up anti-India hysteria in the Muslim world. Today's Urdu paper *Jung* carried an article based on this theory. Can India and Pakistan will ever come together and sit across the table? That question is uppermost in the mind of an average Pakistani. That is possible if there is a democratic Government guaranteeing her subjects the right of free expression and free movement of Indians to Pakistan. If the current trend continues, the anti-India stance will eventually become a part of Pakistan history and any attempt, concerted and coordinated, at a later stage to rewrite history may become virtually impossible.

April 28

The possibility of break in diplomatic relations between India and Pakistan has been hinted in today's newspapers. The consequences of such a drastic step have not perhaps been well gauged by Pakistan, who to all intents and purposes, is determined to blame India for every move. We know what treatment was meted out to Mrs Sen Gupta, the wife of the Deputy High Commissioner in Dacca, at the airport. Pakistan brushed aside India's protest by saying that that was a case of mistaken identity.

The delicate situation of Pakistan economy in general can be judged from the fact that import of all finished products has been banned. This has caused shortages of medicines, books, newsprint, electrical gadgets, etc. and has raised the prices of many items.

The conditions in East Bengal are reported to be very bad. The labourers who had run away to the villages for fear of being killed are afraid of returning to the cities to resume work in the factories and jute mills. A majority of West Pakistani businessmen in East Bengal have either wound up their business there or have sent their wives and children back to West Pakistan. Incidents of killings and murder have created panic among the West Pakistanis living and working in East Bengal.

All commercial activity in East Bengal has come to a standstill. Chittagong port is not working satisfactorily. Jute mills have been damaged and jute cultivation badly affected. Rail links have been cut off and many bridges blown off.

Prices of essential commodities in East Bengal have shot up. Shops do not open regularly. There are not many buyers either.

Bhutto is clamouring for restoration of democratic rights in West Pakistan, while allowing East Pakistan to remain under Martial Law. What a lackadaisical approach to the rights of the Bengali Muslims? East Pakistan is reduced to state of a colony – akin to the protıgı of the British Empire in India. If Pakistan succeeds in her ill-motivated designs, the plight of the Bengalis can be easily construed.

In a country where the entry of impartial foreign observers and correspondents has been banned, one can well imagine with what kind of thoughts and ideas the Pakistanis are being daily fed by the Pakistan media at the behest of the Military Government.

Red Guards said "what is the greatest happiness in the world? To see the face of supreme commander Mao". Pakistani rulers and those who control and run the media seem to say, "What is the greatest happiness in Pakistan? To spite India".

April 29

The weather has been very bad today. The city was enveloped by a thick blanket of dust throughout the day. Did not venture to go out for an evening stroll.

April 30

There is a sudden lull in Pakistan's war of propaganda against India. Anxious to get her people evacuated from her Mission in Calcutta, Pakistan is manipulating a temporary truce with India. The shift in her stand is simultaneously attributed to shift in India's stand towards Pakistan. The implication is that Pakistan does what India does first. In other words, the blame lies entirely with India for the current impasse.

May 1

Bhutto is trying to assert himself and is nosily demanding for restoration of democracy on the basis of elections already held. However, some opposition parties are stoutly opposed to his move for considerations and motives of their own. They are interested in holding fresh elections in which, logically, Bhutto is not interested because he has already a clear majority behind him.

India's open door visa policy has not paid dividends. At least 80% of the people who visit India are illiterate and even if we win their hearts by granting them visas as and when they apply, their goodwill for India has no impact on the body politic of Pakistan. Being illiterate they cannot express themselves effectively through known media. The educated and the businessmen who visit India do not want to say anything in favour of India for fear of annoying the Government of Pakistan. That could also result in cancellation of their passports or a ban on their next visit to India.

Pakistan can go to any length in maligning and implicating India. The latest propaganda is that Indian infiltrators and miscreants in East Bengal have abducted the Bengali girls and looted grain stores. This is obviously to cover up the misdeeds of their own military men who have abducted and raped innocent Bengali girls and destroyed grain by dropping bombs with the object of coercing the Bengalis into submission. The Pakistani media goes on to add that India's hue and cry over the influx of refugees from East Bengal is nothing but a hoax. These refugees, according to Pakistan radio, are none other than infiltrators who run away at the sight of the Pakistan army. It further says that lakhs of poor Indians sleeping on the pavements of Calcutta are mischievously being shown to the world as refugees from East Bengal.

In a press conference a local correspondent asked a Government spokesman that if according to the Government claim the situation in East Bengal was fast returning to normal, would a foreign correspondent be permitted to visit East Bengal. The reply he got was, "Better ask some other question".

In view of the political uncertainty looming large in East Pakistan, thousands of West Pakistanis, working or doing business there, have left East Pakistan with their families. In order to give a semblance of normalcy, the Government of Pakistan won't admit it. But the situation is obvious from the fact that the Government Schools in Karachi in view of limited capacity, have expressed their inability to handle the influx of children of the West Pakistanis coming back from East Pakistan. However, under pressure from the Government, they have reluctantly agreed to take some additional students as far as possible.

In a news conference when a local newsman asked Bhutto if there was a possibility of rupture of diplomatic relations between India and Pakistan, he gave an evasive reply, "Better put this question to the Government as it is their affair. I don't want to meddle in their affairs". Despite his loud protests against the Government for not restoring democracy, he is as much afraid of the Military regime as is a man in the street. He chooses his words carefully and takes pains not to criticize the military regime beyond a point.

Like most Indians the Pakistanis are very fond of chewing betel leaf that comes from East Pakistan. Since the normal trade between the two wings of Pakistan has been disrupted due to political unrest in East Pakistan, the supply of betel leaf has considerably dwindled and during the last two weeks or so there was practically no betel leaf available in Karachi. One Urdu poet by the name of Rais has written a quatrain which when translated into English means somewhat like this: Betel leaf has eventually come from Dacca. In West Pakistan it is a precious commodity. After two months I have tasted betel leaf that has given me a new lease of life". The Urdu version is: Pan ane lage hain Dhake se; yeh bhi aek fazal-e-kibrai hai/ do mahene ke baad aaj Rais; pan khaya to jan aai hai,

May 2

A great majority of women in Pakistan wear the burqa. They are mostly from poor and middle classes. Women belonging to the rich and upper classes prefer to wear sari (although not sanctioned by Islam) as they feel they look more charming and graceful in that kind of dress. Sari was practically unknown among the Muslim women in that part of India before partition. But the Pakistan media has not taken kindly to it. There were some demonstrations in London by Pakistanis against the visiting Pakistan Cricket Team. Among the demonstrators there were some sari-clad women. The English dailies *Morning News* and *Dawn* carried the news highlighting the sari-clad women thereby implying that those women were under the influence of India. Such action was, by implication, unIslamic.

May 5

Of late Bhutto has become more vocal. He is loudly asking for early transfer of power. He is accusing the military regime of mishandling the unrest in East Pakistan. He thinks West Pakistan should not suffer for the sins of one political party, that is, the Awami League of East Pakistan. From the talks he had with newspaper correspondents, the following points emerged:

1. Pakistan's overall economic condition is very bad and is deteriorating day by day.
2. There is complete censorship of news.
3. There is total ban on political activities.
4. Money is being transferred by West Pakistanis living in East Pakistan to third countries and not to West Pakistan.
5. The revolt in East Pakistan is serious.
6. The situation in East Pakistan cannot be handled effectively by the Military regime.
7. In East Pakistan there is mounting economic crisis, acute labour unrest, indiscriminate retrenchment of workers in

factories and mills and ejectment of tenants from the agricultural land.

8. Additional taxation is in the offing to meet the rising cost of military operation in East Pakistan and deployment of troops on the borders with India.
9. Over the equitable distribution of Indus Basin waters there is big dispute among the provinces of Pakistan, that is, the Punjab, Sind, Baluchistan and NWFP.

Bhutto is not in favour of holding fresh elections. He thinks that those calling for fresh elections are 'persons with unpatriotic approach'.

There is acute shortage of newsprint for newspapers. The Government has issued a regulation limiting the size of a newspaper to a maximum of 46 pages in a week with no supplements at all.

Pakistan foreign exchange reserves are dwindling fast. There is a virtual ban on foreign travel even for business purposes. Anybody who wants to travel abroad has to take prior permission of the Government. Virtually every application is rejected.

May 8

Islam plays a decisive role in building up mass hysteria, particularly against India. Connected with religion is blind faith in luck. India is considered to be primarily responsible for all the ills of Pakistan and if India is not, fate is. That means fate is against Pakistan.

But religion has paradoxes. At night I went to see a movie "Our Man Flint", which had a good deal of sex in it. The large sign board outside the cinema hall had been covered with a black cloth because the semi-nude figures painted on it would have hurt the sentiments of the Muslims on the occasion of Id-e-Milad. The house was full.

Somehow the religion in Pakistan is basically meant for the consumption of poor masses that constitute not less than 90% of the total population. The religious card has so far been the trump card with every Government in Pakistan backed by the industrialists and the politicians to keep the poor masses in good humour. If they are poor, that is the will of God. In the name of Islam it is easy and cheap to get the support of the people for any cause, worthy or unworthy.

May 10

Bhutto is becoming restless and more vociferous. He is likely to erupt in hysterical outbursts if his demands are not met. That may create trouble for him because the military regime led by General Yahya Khan, the President of Pakistan, is in no mood to transfer power to him, despite the fact that from time to time he is making false promises and assuring the masses with all the apparent sincerity that he would soon transfer power to the elected representatives. Besides, there are zamindars, industrialists and businessmen, mostly the Punjabi element, who do not want a democratic government for fear of nationalization and curbs on land holdings. Even before partition that part, particularly, the Punjab and Sind, was notorious for having big landlords owning acres and acres of land spread over many villages despite a low density of population. During all the years the Martial Law had been in force they have built up their own small empires. Any change in the administrative set up may add to the economic chaos, they proclaim and pretend. No wonder they support the military regime.

Other than the landlords and the industrialists, there are influential people in the armed forces on whose backing and full support Yahya Khan has to rely. They too would not certainly approve the rule of law as that would deprive them of the power they wield in Pakistan. Last and not the least is the police force. Who would give them the free hand to oppress their people and indulge in corrupt practices, once democracy is back on the wheels?

During all the years the Martial Law has been in force, the big shots in industry, land, the Army and the Police have gradually built up positions and possessions for themselves that have become an integral part of Pakistan economy. Any change (even otherwise least desired and least likely) in the status quo may create chaos and further weaken the economy. That course of reform Pakistan can ill afford at this juncture when conditions in East Pakistan have become chaotic, almost to the point of no return to normalcy and the Military regime is all set and determined to go to war with India.

May 11

The Foreign Exchange position of Pakistan is worsening day by day. The American Banks have refused to accept letters of credit opened by Pakistani importers unless 100% amount is deposited in advance. Japanese and Swiss banks are likely to follow suit.

The bogey of Islam in danger raised by Pakistan has paid some dividends. Saudi Arabia, Turkey and Iran have offered financial help in the form of foreign exchange to enable Pakistan to tide over her present financial crisis. But how much of the foreign exchange comes and how long it lasts that only the future will tell.

All is not well on the eastern front. Daily news that West Pakistan forces have succeeded in maintaining law and order, that business has returned to normal, that factories and ports have started working again, that schools have reopened in East Pakistan, and so on so forth, shows how desperate the Government of Pakistan is to convince her citizens that everything is under control.

The US Senate Foreign Relations Committee has passed a resolution urging Washington to stop deliveries of American arms and ammunition to Pakistan until the conflict in the East Wing ends. Pakistan, as usual, is blaming India for the resolution because of her animosity towards Pakistan. The daily *Dawn* says India has influenced America in her endeavour to exploit Pakistan's difficulties "in accordance with her policy" adopted since the time the two countries became independent in 1947.

May 13

History is being distorted out of proportion. Conscious efforts are being made to advance the names of Muslims responsible for the freedom of India. Maulana Hasrat Mohani is being labelled as the foremost and most conspicuous of all the people in India's struggle for independence. It is being said that even Gandhi in his early life wore foreign clothes, but not the Maulana. Once in London he refused a foreign-made blanket even at the risk of exposing himself to severe cold. Nobody perhaps bothers to ask how he survived in the intense cold of England. Did he carry a razai (cotton filled blanket) with him and for food did he carry rotis with him?

The quality of articles manufactured in Pakistan is very poor. 2221 women have died during the last 16 years (800 in the last 5 years) due to use of defective oil stoves produced in Pakistan, as reported by an Urdu daily. Needless to say, the Government has not taken any action against the manufacturers, and no compensation has been paid to the next of kin of the dead and those who have suffered severe injuries. There is no consumer lobby in the country to protect the basic rights of the consumers. Nor is one liked by the manufacturers and encouraged by the Government.

Pakistan depends on imports from the USA, China, England, Japan, and other countries for her daily needs of even small items like needles, buttons, blades, chinaware and cosmetics besides a large segment of food items. But the imported goods are so costly to be beyond the reach of a common man, whereas the locally produced goods are much below standard.

May 14

Mujib-ul-Rahman, Tajuddin Ahmed and Kamaruddin (all from East Pakistan) are being dubbed by Pakistan as Indian agents, who were sent to East Bengal in 1947 with a view to destroying the ideology of Pakistan and disrupting the life in general. This innovative story has come from Maulvi Farid Ahmed, Vice-President of Pakistan Democratic Party. All sorts of lies are invented to implicate India for anything that goes wrong in Pakistan.

There is shortage of blood plasma. An appeal has been made to the young to donate blood required for sick people, though it is common knowledge that blood is needed for the Pakistani soldiers wounded in East Bengal. An observer says that many young people have sold their blood in order to make both ends meet. In the same breath he says by eating adulterated food, the Pakistani blood had become white. The implication is that the blood donated or sold is contagious.

The problem of the educated unemployed is very acute. It is reported that even students, who got gold medals for outstanding performance in the examinations, cannot get jobs for more than two hundred rupees a month. Out of 7,000 students who were to receive degrees, only 1,000 came to attend the function. Many students are searching for avenues outside Pakistan, but as it is almost impossible to get permission to go abroad, their hopes of settling down in life have been belied.

May 15

In spite of repeated claims made by the Government of Pakistan that all is quiet on the eastern front, off and on, some leaders do come out with the bare facts, whether of their own or motivated by self-interest, it is, of course, hard to say. A seven members delegation sent to East Pakistan to survey the industrial and trade conditions has reported that it would take time before the conditions become stable once again. One Mr. Nur-ul-Amin has categorically stated that it would take at least six months before the factories run to their full capacity. Even Bhutto has said that there was once an annual trade of Rupees 27.5 crore between the two wings, which has almost entirely disappeared. This is one side of the picture. The other side is equally blurred.

The Government of Pakistan is saying time and again that the schools in East Pakistan are getting reopened after an unaccountable break of more than two months, because that is not the time for summer break. That sounds paradoxical and contradictory to the almost daily bulletins issued by the Government that conditions in East Pakistan are normal. If the situation was normal, why were the schools closed in the first instance? The Government is trying to encourage and motivate the West Pakistanis, who came back from East Pakistan a month ago or so, to go again to that wing of Pakistan.

May 16

Pakistan is heavily depending on China for financial aid. So far, China has given 3.07 billion dollars to Pakistan. Two billion dollars were given last year alone. Whether this has been given as a loan or aid or both loan and aid, is not clear. The Government of Pakistan obviously made this statement to tell her people that she has friends in need and that curbs on import of essential commodities would ease soon.

The Pakistan society consists of haves and have-nots. The haves are the lucky high officials in the bureaucracy and the armed forces, the businessmen and the landowners.

The wives of high government and military officers are reported to have imported cosmetics on medical prescriptions, whereas there are large areas in Pakistan without a single Government dispensary and there are no records of the sick and the old who have died for want of medicines. The doctors employed in Government hospitals are not interested in going to villages and remote areas of Pakistan. The consultation fees charged by private doctors are beyond the reach of common people. The situation is getting worse day by day.

The Government is in a tight corner. If the costly operations in East Pakistan continue, the situation may further deteriorate bringing Pakistan on the verge of economic collapse. The symptoms of acute unemployment or people being thrown out of employment are coming to the surface. The reasons are not too far to seek. There is virtually no trade, and no exports. The import of raw materials having been drastically cut down, the industrial units are lying idle. That may be detrimental to the already poor household budget of an ordinary worker. An average industrialist is sitting tight because he has sufficient assets and amassed wealth to last him for at least the next generation.

May 18

Pakistan is looking for resources to meet the foreign exchange crisis. The Government is trying to get aid from Muslim countries – Saudi Arabia, Kuwait and states in the Persian Gulf. She is expecting two million dollars aid from Saudi Arabia and the rest from others. Two non-governmental delegations consisting of industrialists and businessmen, who are stated to have connections with the rulers of these states, are likely to be sent there.

It is mentioned in some circles that the aid promised by China is still to materialize. In this distorted economic scenario to know the exact position or the truth is not an easy task. Earlier some newspapers did mention that some aid had already come from China.

A large number of West Pakistanis have returned from East Pakistan with their wives and children because of disturbed conditions and uncertain future. Even those Muslims who had originally migrated from Bihar, U.P. and other parts of India to East Pakistan have come to West Pakistan. No West Pakistani is interested in going back to East Pakistan at the risk of his very life.

May 19

We, the members of the Indian High Commission, are virtually prisoners here. If anyone wants to visit India, the High Commission has to seek the permission of the Government of Pakistan. One of our members wanted to visit Delhi because his father was seriously ill. He was refused permission. His father meanwhile expired and until this day he has not been allowed to leave Karachi. It is paradoxical that whereas we are issuing visas to thousands of Pakistanis to visit India, we ourselves cannot go. The members of a Diplomatic Mission are otherwise considered to be in a privileged position; it is just the reverse here.

I was the last person to join the High Commission here. All postings after me have been frozen. Those who think that the Foreign Service is synonymous with diplomatic postings to New York, London, Sydney, Ottawa and Tokyo should not forget there are places like Karachi where we are living on borrowed times subject to the whims of the Government of Pakistan.

Sometimes I feel lonely and sad. I had accepted Karachi thinking that I would be taking my wife and two sons Anil and Vinay with me because educational facilities in the medium of English were available here. Secondly we would be so close to India that if I wanted to send Anil to a higher secondary school in Delhi or elsewhere, that would pose no problem. I had also a desire to visit Muzaffargarh, 250 miles from Karachi, where I was born; but in the wake of the partition of the British India into India and Pakistan, my family was forced to migrate to India. I could neither bring my family here not visit my native place. If I had delayed my departure for one week, I would not have come here at all.

The Ministry of External Affairs wanted to cut down the size of our Missions in Islamabad and Karachi in West Pakistan, and Dacca and Rajshai in East Pakistan, but the Government of Pakistan did not give permission to a single man to leave. Obviously in the event of war, they want to keep us as hostages so as to be in a strong position later on to bargain with India.

Life in West Pakistan in the sense of law and order situation seems normal mostly because the West Pakistanis have been successfully kept in the dark about happenings in East Pakistan. Some may have a vague idea of the unrest there, but they have no means of getting a complete picture. An economic crisis of higher magnitude is approaching fast. Out of sheer desperation Pakistan is now condemning and abusing all countries except China and the Muslim countries. She is accusing America and Western countries of playing into the hands of India in regard to political turmoil in East Pakistan. It sounds so absurd. But unfortunately absurdity has become a part of life in Pakistan.

May 22

Pakistan never slackens her anti-India propaganda. Even Yahya Khan finds it convenient to blame India. In a speech delivered yesterday he says the figure of the refugees from East Pakistan to West Bengal has been inflated by adding the unemployed and the homeless in West Bengal. He adds that instead of treating the question of genuine refugees on humanitarian basis, a callous campaign has been launched by India to exploit the issue for political gains. He does not stop here; he goes on inflaming the passions of Muslims in India so that riots may break out in India which would provide a smoke screen to the atrocities committed by Pakistani soldiers in East Pakistan. He says it is ironical that India has never bothered to show concern for millions of Indian Muslims who have been driven out of their homes and compelled to seek refuge in Pakistan (as if Pakistan's borders with India are so porous that any Indian Muslim can enter Pakistan any time he wants and as if any Indian Muslim is welcome in Pakistan). He does not talk of millions of Hindus and Sikhs who were driven out of Pakistan by violent mobs backed by the Police and the Military soon after the partition.

The issue of Muslims of India seeking refuge in Pakistan has been deliberately raised so that if and when later on the question of taking back Hindu refugees from East Pakistan arises, Pakistan can equate the two and thus refuse to take back the Hindu refugees.

May 23

While Bhutto is trying hard to get power transferred to the elected representatives, the Government is in no mood to oblige him. Bhutto does not figure anywhere on the agenda of Yahya Khan that is heavily loaded with settling scores with India. Perhaps Yahya Khan thinks Bhutto is like a barking dog. With too much barking he will eventually get exhausted and retreat to his solitary den.

Since Bhutto has already got inkling that the military regime is in no mood to transfer power to him, he has sent two emissaries namely A. H.Kardar and Mahamud Ali Kasuri to East Pakistan to win the support of the elected representatives of the defunct Awami League. All sorts of inducements are being offered to them to join the Pakistan Peoples' Party of Bhutto. The atmosphere in East Pakistan is so surcharged with distrust and suspicion of West Pakistan that both the emissaries are bound to return empty handed.

Certain students and politicians are still rotting in Pakistani jails. Dr. Rashid Hussain, a student leader has been in jail for the last 18 months without trial. The Pakistani newspapers, though claiming to be independent and impartial, are scared of publishing the names of the students in Pakistani jails.

The prices of essential commodities are going up day by day. It is feared rationing may be introduced. Many factories are lying idle for want of raw materials and many are running to their half capacity. Smuggling is on the increase to avoid taxation and excise and custom duties. Corruption is rampant. It is said that corrupt Government servants and black-marketers and law-breakers get punished on paper only. On appeals, sentences are drastically cut and fines considerably reduced. The judgements of the appellate courts are not reported in the press to keep the public ignorant of the reality.

It is a well-known fact that no Pakistani can get a passport unless he bribes the officials to the extent of rupees two hundred fifty to three hundred per passport. The funny thing is that in a majority of cases the validity of the passport is restricted to one year only though its normal expiry period is five years. The idea is that after the expiry of the passport, the holder will have to come again to renew the passport and thus bribe the officials once more for the same service. Similarly, foreign exchange is released only to those who are either influential or can bribe the Government officials.

May 25

Who will believe Yahya Khan when he says, "It is self-censorship, no censorshipis imposed on the press" in Pakistan. If the Military regime had given freedom of expression to the press, truth would not have remained hidden so long.

Yaha Khan has proposed to transfer power to the elected representatives in two to three months time. Will he? That is a million dollar question. He may. He may not. He may, because Pakistan is on the brink of economic collapse; he will get rid of the trouble of reconstructing the economy. He may not because he is under tremendous pressure from the army top brass. Perhaps he is riding on the horns of a dilemma. The damage has been done. It will need gigantic efforts to bring Pakistan's economy back to the pre-East Pakistan debacle.

Anti-India propaganda does appear to have a desired impact on the masses in general, who are mostly illiterate. However, there are some voices, largely among the educated classes who do apparently believe in a rational approach. They do want amity between India and Pakistan, but unfortunately they are in a poor minority with no outlet to express their views and opinions.

May 26

Pakistan is much worried about her economy. It seems no significant help is coming from the Muslim countries on whose support Pakistan was banking so much. Even aid from China is not substantial, though Pakistan has taken great pains in eulogizing China for her timely help. Pakistan cannot expect any aid from the Non-Muslim countries because on the Bangladesh issue, she has slandered them for their criticism and advice beyond a reasonable degree of tolerance.

May 28

The delicate state of Pakistan's economy can be judged from the fact that the import of finished goods has been banned. Efforts are being made to produce things in Pakistan. But, as it is, other than anti-India propaganda things cannot be manufactured in Pakistan overnight. This has caused acute shortage of medicines, newsprint, electrical items, books, etc and has steeply raised the prices of many commodities.

The conditions in East Pakistan are still chaotic. The workers who had run away from the cities and towns to the villages for fear of being killed or coerced by the Army to work, despite no means of subsistence, are afraid of coming back to resume work in the factories and the mills. In spite of persuasions and pleas by the Government of Pakistan, those West Pakistanis who had come back to West Pakistan to save their lives, are refusing to go back. Incidents of daily murders and killings have created panic among the West Pakistanis and those Muslims who migrated direct from the States of Bihar, UP and Assam in India to East Pakistan and are still left in East Pakistan. Once they knowingly and willingly opted for Pakistan, they cannot go back to India and they are surely afraid of going to West Pakistan because they do not know what fate they would meet there.

Moreover, as all means of link by road or rail through India and by sea from Dacca or Chittagong to Karachi stand cut off or suspended, more than 95% of the people in East Pakistan cannot afford to go to West Pakistan by air which is so costly. Since the Pakistani planes cannot fly over India they have to take a longer route that has substantially increased the fare.

All commercial activity in East Pakistan is at standstill. Chittagong Port is working in a lopsided fashion. Most of the jute mills have been damaged and the jute cultivation is badly affected. Rail links have been cut off and many bridges blown off.

Prices of essential commodities in East Pakistan have skyrocketed. For instance, sugar is being sold at rupees ten per ṣeer against the normal price of rupees two. Shops do not open regularly and even if they open, there are not many customers. The purchasing power of the common man has been unbelievably eroded.

May 29

Does Pakistan really want no war with India, as made out by the Pakistan media? She may not at this moment when her hands are full with controlling the uprising in East Pakistan. But she will not spare us as and when she thinks she is in a position to strike us.

Film actors and actresses are still looked down upon by the Islamic society in Pakistan. New talent is difficult to get. It is learnt that most of the directors and producers consider actresses as their keeps or mistresses. Because of the sexy scenes and raw vulgar humour the Punjabi films are more popular than those in Urdu and Sindhi.

The daughter of Malika Pukhraj, a very famous singer, particularly of the Urdu gazals, on the TV today sang Hafiz Jullundhry's popular poem 'Abhi To Mein Jawan Hun' (I am still young). Since I have also heard Malika Pukhraj, her daughter's voice is not that melodious.

Religious bigotry can go to any length. One Dr. Basharat Ali speaking on the Pakistani population, its problems and solutions says, "The rise in population is on God's command. He will provide food. The birth control system has come from the countries across the sea. It has been deliberately introduced in Pakistan and other Muslim countries to reduce the Muslims so that entire Muslim race could be annihilated in course of time".

There is inordinate delay in the disposal of criminal and civil cases by the Pakistani courts, though majority of criminal cases under the Martial Law cannot be taken to the regular courts. The delay is attributed to large number of suits, the faulty legal system, dearth of judges, and the defective methods of recording evidence and investigation of crimes.

There is not only shortage of seats in schools, there is also acute shortage of text books. This is attributed partly to the sudden return of West Pakistani families from East Pakistan and shortage of printing paper.

The general knowledge of an average student is pathetic. In a test the answers to some simple questions were grotesque.

Q Where is the naval headquarters of Nepal?
A Kathmandu.
Q If you are facing the sun, what direction is on your left?
A West.
Q How many islands Philippines has?
A 600.
Q How many times Muhammad's name comes in Quran?
A (silence)

This gist appeared on the television.

May 30

Pakistani press seems to have lost any sense of discrimination and decency. Commenting on J.P. Narayan's visit to Arab countries, a writer by the name of Nasurula Khan writes in *Hurriat*. "When J.P. Narayan went to Arab countries they asked him – How is Golda Meir? J.P. replied – I am not from Israel, but from India. The Arabs said – It is a difference of name only. Israel and Bharat are the same. Indira Gandhi is the Bharti name of Golda Meir." What does this imply? Are the Arabs so ignorant as not to know the difference between Indira Gandhi and Golda Meir? Or, the story was concocted by the writer. The latter seems more plausible.

A few days ago same newspaper said, "Sardar Swaran Singh has no brain. He has, however, two wives." By implication he meant Indira Gandhi was his second wife. The same story was repeated about Jagjivan Ram.

It is again a neurotic approach when the Editor of the same newspaper talks of poverty, unemployment, etc. in India, while the Muslims in Pakistan are in a worse plight. He says, "In a country (India) where most of 55 crore people are suffering from hunger, nakedness and poverty and whose main problems are bread, clothes, employment, education, medical facilities and shelter, it is not clear how she is preparing for war". He goes on to add, "If India tries to improve relations with China and Pakistan instead of becoming mad, it can change the whole of Asia because instead of spending money on arms and ammunition, we can improve the lot of our people". It sounds like a rogue giving advice to a gentleman. It is as if Pakistan is a highly developed country and has a great sympathy for India. Whom is the Editor trying to befool? Obviously, the people of Pakistan.

May 31

Karachi is a city of crimes. Abduction of girls, rapes, murders and traffic accidents are quite common. Reckless driving of buses and heavy vehicles has been the cause of many deaths.

It is rumoured that instead of handing over power to the elected representatives, Yahya Khan may form an advisory council. Another instance of feeding people on false promises and thus throwing dust into their eyes.

Khan Wali Khan's resignation from the party stems from his disgust and disenchantment with the political life in Pakistan. After so many years of martial law, people had hoped for return of democracy, but all their hopes have been dashed to the ground by Yahya Khan.

June 1

Taking full advantage of the strained relations between India and Pakistan, China is obviously exploiting the situation to her advantage both politically and economically. By extending credit to Pakistan, China is creating a market for her consumer goods, which cannot be easily sold in the world market because of stiff competition from Japan, USA, UK and other commercial giants.

But China is unlikely to extend long term credit to Pakistan for plant and machinery, as she would perhaps like to watch how the Pakistan economy develops. That means whether Pakistan would be in a position to pay back the loan money because any investment in long term projects not only requires large funds but also, in the ultimate analysis, making Pakistan self-dependent thus dispensing with her dependence on China.

Some prosperity, which Ayub Khan brought to Pakistan in early years, has been frittered away in importing luxury goods for the rich landlords, businessmen and top military brass and bureaucrats. One of the reasons why Pakistan did not pay much attention to set up an industrial base in the country is that she was making easy money by exporting jute from East Pakistan and utilizing the foreign exchange earned for imports into West Pakistan. It is estimated 70% of foreign exchange came through export of raw jute and jute products.

It is reliably learnt that more and more troops, particularly from Quetta, Multan and even Lahore and Karachi have been sent to East Pakistan where the situation is getting out of control. The number of soldiers killed so far has been kept a secret. Unconfirmed reports say that there are large casualties among the soldiers. Of course, these are fewer than the civilian casualties. It is natural because the civilians being unarmed are much more vulnerable.

June 2

Sheikh Mujib-ur-Rehman is reported to be on hunger strike in jail. Nobody is allowed to see him. There are no reports on his health and his general condition.

The Government of Pakistan has stepped up playing of national songs with warlike overtones on radio and television to mislead people into believing that India is preparing to attack Pakistan and Pakistan has to keep herself in readiness. It suits the agenda of the Government so that the people do not raise a hue and cry against rising costs of essential consumer goods, unemployment and denial of fundamental rights, whatever these are.

Prices of essential commodities like sugar, tobacco, edible oils, vanaspati, and other items of daily use have gone up by 50 to 100%. A matchbox that earlier cost 6 paisa now costs 15 paisa. Most of the commodities, the prices of which have gone up, have disappeared from the market. Popular brands of ghee, medicines and packed goods are not available except at high cost in black market. In the early days of martial law, shopkeepers were afraid of selling goods at higher price, but with the passage of time, they care two hoots for the government, although they do not say it openly.

It is reported that the Government is planning to allot barren land to the agitated farmers in Punjab where most of the agricultural products including wheat, rice and sugarcane are grown. It is an eye wash. What will a farmer do with the barren land without water, seeds and agricultural tools? Where will the money come from? The Government does not extend any loan to the farmers and the banks have already closed their doors to them.

The Government is publishing exaggerated records of national production to mislead the public into thinking that the economy is strong and all is well.

In an editorial the *Urdu* daily *Hurriat* mentions that while the Government of Pakistan has removed censorship on dispatches sent by the foreign correspondents, the same facility has not been extended to the local newspapers which are still subject to heavy censorship. Either the news is not correct or the management is trying to mislead its readers. The foreign correspondents are not free to send dispatches back home.

June 3

It is learnt that 40,000 policemen (10,000 from Karachi and 30,000 from Quetta and other places) are being sent to East

Pakistan to release the pressure on the army for maintaining law and order. Some are being sent by air, others by sea. The Army Police is manning the positions in the cities and big towns.

Crime is on the increase as reported by the vernacular newspapers. Girls are being abducted in broad daylight. Rowdy elements have a free hand. The situation is likely to deteriorate, as there is hardly any trained police force to maintain law and order. The army police, in general, is not trained to handle the civilians and is not familiar with the topography of the cities and the towns. A police constable is reported to have murdered his wife in the court because she had instituted divorce proceedings against him.

Pakistan Intelligence (called CID) does not spare anyone. A man, who was on our mailing list for *India Weekly* issued by the High Commission, has written a pathetic letter requesting us to remove his name from the mailing list as he is being harassed and questioned if he has any links with the High Commission. Outside the Chancery building, CID men present in plain clothes invariably question any Pakistani visiting Indian High Commission. If any visitor, in their opinion, spends longer time than what they think is reasonable, they again question him on his coming out of the building. Harassing their own people every day has become a routine feature of the police and the intelligence men. They are also found snooping around our residences.

In spite of anti-India propaganda there has been no decline in the number of visa applications. This trend shows people in general are not deterred by the media reports that Pakistani visitors in India are not only unwelcome but are also not safe. People have their own ways of verifying the truth. Usually they get the truth from the Pakistanis who return from India after completing their trips or through other sources.

June 5

In spite of anti-India stance adopted by the Government of Pakistan, most Indian things appeal to the masses. The students prefer to read books by Indian authors. The people like to see Indian movies (when visiting India or Afghanistan) and listen to Indian film songs. The films produced in Pakistan are not only of poor quality and but quite often also in bad taste. These are almost carbon copies of popular Indian movies. Even T.V. programmes are no exception. One Pakistani commenting on Pakistan TV programmes writes to the editor of an English Daily *Morning News* that the direction reminds him of old Indian pictures.

The Pakistanis also like to read Indian magazines especially in Urdu because the standard of local newspapers and periodicals is very poor. But for fear of prosecution nobody expresses these preferences openly. This reminds me an incident that happened with me. One of our officers had imported a Television set for which he had the prior approval and permission of the Foreign Office of Pakistan. But the Customs would not release it without giving any cogent reason. Whenever the officer sent his assistant to get the TV, the Customs Officer used delaying tactics on one pretext or another, for example, the TV has been misplaced or the storekeeper is absent today and so on and so forth. The officer said to me, "Since you are in charge of issuing visas, may be you have some influence with the Customs". I said that I would try. Next day accompanied by my assistant I went to the Customs Office. When I introduced myself, the Customs Officer became courteous and offered me a seat, but in the same breath he said, "You are not giving visas these days"' I replied, "That is not true. We have some restrictions. That is all. But for you or your people, there is no bar. If anyone you recommend has a problem, send him to me."

The Customs Officer talked to his subordinate on the phone and advised us to collect the TV from him. His subordinate Bashir Khan received us warmly and said to me, "Sir, in the past your people used to give us cigarettes and Urdu magazines but these days nobody gives anything". I replied, "I can still give you some. But you know the situation these days is very bad. If someone sees you taking cigarettes and magazines from me, you will be in trouble. Nobody will say anything to me because I have diplomatic immunity". Bashir suggested with a faint smile, "When you come tomorrow, put the cigarettes and the magazines in a bag. Leave it here. I will empty the contents and will call you back saying that you have forgotten your bag". Next day I did exactly as he had suggested. I put a carton of State Express 555 cigarettes and a few old Urdu magazines picked up from the shelves of our large library (now almost defunct because nobody comes to read) and he did exactly what he had agreed to. Thus I managed to get the TV released. Literate Muslims no doubt enjoy reading Urdu poetry and fiction.

There had been looting of currency notes in East Pakistan recently. The Government of Pakistan spared no effort in assigning blame to infiltrators from India. But now gradually looted currency notes are being recovered from the West Pakistanis. The Government is trying to investigate how this happened.

One Pakistani writer Ibrahim Jalees commenting on the goondas (bad element like rogues and scoundrels) of Lahore feels pride in the so-called fact that before partition all goondas of India trembled at the sight of a Lahori goonda. So far as Pakistan is concerned the presence of these goondas is an evil besides a law and order problem, but when it comes to India it is a matter of pride.

June 7

Pakistan has demonetized Rs 500 and Rs 100 currency notes.

It is learnt that feelers are being thrown to Mujib-ur-Rahman to compromise with Military regime. A Herculean task indeed!

There is growing discontentment among the labour class because of retrenchment of workers and steep rise in the prices of essential commodities making it difficult for a worker to make both ends meet. Perhaps the factory owners are equally helpless. The production has fallen due to shortage of raw materials mostly imported and the exports have fallen because of low production and disturbed conditions in East Pakistan.

June 11

Demonetization of currency has become the most burning question. Various kinds of rumours and speculations have started circulating. The Government has ultimately come out with an offer of compensation upto a deposit of Rs 1,000 only. For any sum above Rs 1,000 a committee will sit on judgement. The Government cannot afford to print more currency notes. Rs 2,000 crore worth of currency notes have already been printed during the last two years. The people have legitimate apprehensions if they will be compensated for the demonetized currency.

Everybody except a beggar stands crushed. There are no marriages and thus no parties. No functions are allowed. Majority of the people cannot travel even within the country because they have no money to spare. Even business is doomed. For three consecutive days, stock exchanges and bullion markets throughout the country were closed.

It is strongly rumoured that even Rs 50 currency notes may be demonetized. Shopkeepers are reluctant to accept a note of that denomination either. Only notes of rupees ten, five and one are acceptable tender.

Unaccounted money or black money has been reportedly destroyed by the hoarders. Nobody will risk depositing it with the banks and face serious consequences under the martial law regulations. Banks even otherwise would not accept currency notes of higher denomination. One person threw notes into a dirty nullah and many passersby, not caring for the dirt and the stinking smell, jumped into it to retrieve as much as possible. Only the lucky got notes of rupees fifty and below which are the legal tender

Borders with India, Afghanistan and Iran were sealed for three days to prevent outflow of Pakistan money. Incoming and outgoing passengers were subjected to severe checking at the ports. It is learnt these measures were taken by the Government to unearth looted currency notes from East Pakistan, and to deduct cases of income tax evasion.

But the fact is that the Government had already become bankrupt and had no money to pay even salaries for the month of May. During the last two years Pakistan has overprinted currency to the tune of Rupees 2,000 crore. Any further printing would lead to further inflationary pressure. The Government had to demonetize currency in circumstances beyond her control. The business community and the industry put lot of pressure on the Government not to take the extreme step, but the Government had no alternative. The exchequer was empty. It is said that the money collected from the people on the promise of compensation would keep the Government running for some time.

It is acknowledged in business circles that Pakistan has not yet fully recovered from the after effects of 1965 war with India, when a new trouble of greater magnitude (turmoil in East Pakistan) with serious economic consequences has raised its ugly head. The costly operations in East Pakistan have resulted in total disruption of trade between the two wings and even with the outside world.

June 13

Feroze Abdullah, who killed Polish Deputy Foreign Minister Mr.Wolniah and three Pakistanis on November 1 last year, was hanged yesterday morning. It is surprising the newspapers, particularly vernacular, have given the event wide coverage elevating Feroze to the status of a martyr. Fanaticism and religious bigotry has a wider and sensational appeal to the masses.

June 14

Khan Abdul Ghaffar Khan, popularly known as the Frontier Gandhi, says in his autobiography,"Pakistan was founded on hatred.

She was born not out of love, but of hatred and she grew up on hatred, on malice, on spite and on hostility". He continues, "Pakistan is unable to think in terms of peace and friendship. She wants to keep the Pakistani people under control by making them live in a nightmare of riots, assaults and holy war."

What he said many years ago, the events of subsequent years have proved it true. The genocide in East Pakistan has perhaps few parallels in history. The sowing of seeds of hatred against India too has few parallels in history.

June 15

Pakistan is trying to tell the world that all is well with her economy. The reality is totally different. Factories even in West Pakistan are not running in full shifts. Commercial and trade activity has come to a standstill because access to East Pakistan, which absorbed more than 50% of goods manufactured in West Pakistan, is virtually blocked. For all her economic ills Pakistan is making India a scapegoat. Pakistani media never gets tired of blaming India for every problem of Pakistan. In an article in an Urdu daily on Indian Hindus the writer concludes: "India is directly responsible for the current situation in Pakistan. But there is also an international conspiracy against all the Muslim countries. In East Asia the work has been entrusted to the Israeli Jews. Here it has been entrusted to the Indian Hindu Government. All enemies of Pakistan are siding with India"

The businessmen and industrialists are putting pressure on the Government to compensate people against demonetized currency upto Rs 10,000 per person. It is doubtful if the Government will oblige. Curtailment of buying power through demanetization of currency with virtually no compensation has considerably slowed down production causing mounting anxiety to the industrialists and the businessmen alike. Had not some Muslim countries for partisan considerations particularly in the Gulf come to the rescue of Pakistan, the country would have broken up by now.

The Government has appointed a committee to examine each case of compensation for demonetized currency on merits. But people have genuine fears that the deliberations of the committee will take such a long time that people will forget about it. Nothing will come out of nothing. Harder days are in store for most of the Pakistanis especially the common man.

June 18

The workers in factories and business establishments are being retrenched or being forced to proceed on half pay leave as commercial and industrial activity has considerably become sluggish. The supplies to East Pakistan have still not been resumed. Textile and sugar mills are the worst affected.

Though there is no curfew in Dacca, people are afraid of coming out of their houses at night. Non-Bengalis, mostly from West Pakistan are afraid of going to localities inhabited by the Bengalis. They are scared by sheer numbers, who are up in arms against the military regime firmly entrenched in West Pakistan.

It is learnt that many soldiers from West Pakistan have been injured and are hospitalized in East Pakistan. Though the hospitals are full, the injured are not being sent back to West Pakistan for fear of creating panic among the West Pakistanis. Another reason could be Pakistan has transportation problems. The Army has to send additional troops and supplies through planes that have to take a circuitous route as they cannot fly over Indian territory. It is undoubtedly an expensive operation too.

It is learnt that when the big business got news through corrupt officials that the Government was contemplating a total ban on the import of manufactured articles due to worsening foreign exchange position, they placed maximum orders for the imported goods, which they are holding back in their godowns in the expectation of making higher profits when the availability of the goods become scarce.

Much of the financial aid from China, Kuwait and Persian Gulf countries is still eagerly awaited. A ship supposed to bring newsprint paper to Karachi a few days ago has still not arrived. Another ship carrying merchandise from East Pakistan has not come. Two ships carrying merchandise from West Pakistan have not reached Chittagong. Where have these ships disappeared? Nobody knows. Some people think this is all propaganda by the Government of Pakistan that things are normal.

June 19

Professor Ghulam Azam of Jamat-e-Islami, talking to news correspondents in Lahore has revealed that the situation in East Pakistan is not normal. Underground activities are continuing and the opponents of military regime target anybody supporting or openly expressing loyalty to the Government of Pakistan operating from Islamabad. They are receiving encouragement from Naxalites and leftist organizations, within and outside the country. The Bengali separatists are still in control of remote villages forcibly stopping anybody listening to Radio Pakistan. The peace committees set up by martial law authorities with the objective of maintaining harmony between the Bengalis and the Non-Bengalis have proved ineffective, as they are not able to restore confidence among the people. There is panic and fear everywhere.

A proposal has been made by the Pakistan Government think-tank to divide East Pakistan into three administrative units for easy governance. That may further upset the Bengalis by adding fuel to the fire. Every possible effort is being made to maintain the hold on East Pakistan.

It is reported that by the Government account on June 7, Rupees 831 crore were in circulation of which Rupees 460 were in the form of currency notes of Rupees 500 and 100. Only Rupees 360 crore have been deposited with banks. The balance remains unaccounted. Either the remaining money in the form of black money is in the hands of corrupt Government Officials and business community or some of it has been destroyed to avoid raids by the Income Tax Office.

Time and again businessmen and traders are complaining that compensation of Rupees 1,000 in lieu of demonetized currency is not at all sufficient to conduct any meaningful business. It is not even enough to pay income tax and meet day-to-day expenses on maintaining household and business establishments.

Rumours on further devaluation of Pakistan currency are afloat. It is learnt that foreign aid is contingent on the devaluation of Pakistan currency.

Except for the news that Tikka Khan was killed in action and Mujib-ur-Rahman went underground and an odd news here and there, the news on Bangladesh (East Pakistan) given by AIR and Indian Newspapers has been correct to the maximum extent. It is confirmed from four different sources that two lakh people in East Bengal have been killed in military operations. The armed forces are being harassed by Mukti Bahni (independent Bangla Deshi forces, comprising mostly of Bengali deserters from Pakistan Army and veterans and loyalists to Mujib-ur-Rahman).

Three British Members of Parliament on tour of Pakistan gave a talk on Pakistan Radio last night. Only those portions that basically suit the Government have been published by the newspapers. The MPs have appealed to President Yahya Khan to let foreign correspondents visit East Pakistan and publish the TRUTHS.

The problem of educated unemployed especially of women in Pakistan is not only very acute but also pathetic. One Amina Begum, M.Sc. from Peshawar says she stitches clothes from daybreak till late at night to make both ends meet. She wanted to become an MBBS, but in spite of first division in F.Sc. she could not get admission to a Medical College. One M.A. says that he has not been able to get a job for four years. All these years he was dependent on his sister. He does not specify how his sister is making a living, but he says he is worried because once she gets married, he does not know how he will live. Technical education is available to the boys and girls from affluent families and those who have a rapport with the Government (Martial Law) authorities.

The bureaucrats and military brass do not want to give democratic rights to the people. They say the masses are illiterate and thus incapable of making judgement on political and economic issues. But that is eyewash. The truth is they will be exposed for their nefarious activities such as making illegal gains and leading a luxurious life at the cost of the common man, if they give freedom of expression to the people. Yahya Khan and his cronies are no better than Ayub Khan and his henchmen. There are some right thinking people who feel Pakistan is treading a wrong path by maligning India and killing her own people in East Pakistan. But before guns and bullets they are helpless.

Rumours are in circulation that Yahya Khan is not keeping good health and may be forcibly removed. As a matter of fact Yahya Khan with the East Pakistan debacle looming large before him, wants to quit provided he is given a safe position assuring all the privileges that a ruling President has. The military junta, which has got better hold of Yahya Khan, may not like to kick him out as long as he does what he is told. If he falters, he falls. And knowing the fate of Ayub Khan he would not like to fall.

June 20

One Mr. Hamid-ul-Haq, a former Member of Parliament, has admitted that conditions in East Pakistan are so chaotic as to be beyond any redemption. He adds that West Pakistan cannot understand the loss, both material and emotional, suffered by East Pakistanis.

Pakistani newspapers have started prominently displaying news regarding India's preparedness for war against Pakistan in order to justify her own military action in East Pakistan and abrogation of fundamental rights. Obviously, the feedback has come from the top.

Efforts are being made by Pakistan to pay back her international debts in Pakistan currency. But who will accept Pakistan currency when at this juncture it has absolutely no value in the international market? This is nothing but a freak of Pakistan pious thinking. Moreover, from where will Pakistan get so much of her own currency? By printing more, perhaps by digging into history and taking a cue from the Japanese who widely printed their currency and distributed it in Burma and other territories under their occupation during the Second World War. Pakistan hopes to dig itself out of the hole.

June 22

Although Pakistan prides herself on 1965 war with India by proclaiming with the beat of a drum that she gave a crushing defeat to India, the fact is that her own economy suffered so much and caused great political instability from the after effects of which she has not been able to recover until this day. Why she is preparing for another war with India is anybody's guess? But to cover up her dirty designs on India, she is at the same time appealing to the world powers to restrain India as if it is India that wants war with Pakistan. Pakistan has already exhausted some of her military resources in stemming the tide of rising nationalism among the Bengali Muslims in East Pakistan through violence and barbarity. Hundreds of innocent and unarmed Bengalis have faced the bullets and died. The appeal to the world powers to restrain India is reflected in newspapers editorials that have recently appeared. The *Morning News* in its editorial says, "In the interest of peace, the international community must intervene and put pressure on New Delhi to stop acting in an aggressive manner against this country". Earlier it says, "Pakistan is far too occupied with her internal problems to think of embarking on an adventure which will further ruin its economy and deepen the present crisis". Perhaps the editorial also reflects Pakistan's anxiety about the economic consequences of the war without giving up the idea of war.

The question is if Pakistan feels strongly that, in the event of war with India, her economy will be ruined, why she continues with her malicious propaganda against India? Is it signaling to its intentions with a heavy dose of taxation scheduled to be announced on June 26 and its justification for the additional burden on the people to be put before the nation by Yahya Khan in a televised address scheduled on June 29?

Pakistan's fabrication of sensational and awful stories has no end. Can anyone believe that minority Hindus living in East Pakistan killed Muslims in that part of the country in the present turmoil?

June 24

The manner in which the economists have painted a rosy picture of Pakistan's economy for the year 1970-71 is remarkable. In spite of floods and a devastating cyclone and widespread disturbances in East Pakistan and drought in West Pakistan, they claim that the overall picture is encouraging; no damage has been done to basic economic structure and all jolts to economy have been absorbed.

Nationalization of banks and insurance is very much in the air. This step is considered necessary to utilize large bank deposits in the form of Rupees 500 and 100 currency notes for governmental purposes.

June 27

Pakistan economy has been in a shambles ever since her costly operations in East Pakistan. The fact that every Government servant including those in the armed forces drawing a salary of Rs 500 or above will draw his next increment either in the form of a defense bond or by increasing his contribution to his provident fund shows fissures in Pakistan economy. This step has been taken to freeze cash payments to Government employees, and also to tell the public that they are not the only ones being affected by new budget proposals; even Government servants have not been spared.

Due to death, desertion and dismissal of a large number of Bengalis serving in the Pakistan civil and military services, there have been quick promotions in every department of the Government thus increasing the burden on West Pakistan when there is no revenue from the East Wing. This measure may lead to discontentment among the armed forces. But do they have a choice? Were there is a civilian Government, the armed forces might have revolted and taken charge of the country. In the present situation when a general is the head of the country, what can the disgruntled army men do?

When Mr. M.M. Ahmed, Economic Adviser to the President, tells the nation that like all Pakistanis it is his passionate belief that Pakistan came into existence under a divine scheme and therefore "despite many tribulations and crises is bound to emerge as a strong country which we trust will be a source of strength also to the Muslim world," he is using the best ruse to hoodwink the illiterate people into a belief that whatever has happened so far is due to the will of God and the people of Pakistan will have to make more sacrifices to please God so that His glory and mercy may ultimately bless this nation.

Ever since the creation of Pakistan the people have been led to a belief that God is responsible for all that is good and all that is bad (there is nothing man can do about it) in this country and God has created new India in the form of a Satan for beguiling Pakistan. Perhaps unlike Muslims in other parts of the world, the Pakistani Muslims have a staunch belief that whatever good or bad happens, it is the will of God. In other words, man (a Pakistani Muslim) is in no way responsible and answerable for the ills of the society. Knowing the innate faith of a Muslim in the will of God, the unscrupulous people in society like big landlords, industrialists, businessmen and civilians and now men in armed forces, have fully exploited the poor masses for their selfish gains.

The question is whether God will really help a nation where a brother is killing brother, where women have practically no rights of their own, where rapes and murders are a daily routine affair, where Government officials are corrupt, where the armed forces have ruthlessly killed and maimed their Bengali Muslim brethren in East Pakistan and whose officers have built fortunes for themselves, where the elite roll in luxury and the poor rot in misery, where students are summarily thrown into prison for claiming fundamental rights and are virtually thrown into gutters after spending so much on education and where there is so much of class exploitation, and where minorities in bare minimum numbers are treated like second hand citizens? Only God can answer.

This nation as it seems to live on religious fanaticism should be a lesson to India to remain vigilant and spare no effort to counteract Pakistan's vicious and malicious propaganda against her.

Despite all the poverty and misery and mayhem of innocent men, women and children in East Wing, Pakistan does not want to keep her own version of Islam confined to her frontiers. The religious leaders (mullahs and maulvis) backed by the Government of Pakistan have misled people into a belief that Pakistan is a source of inspiration to the entire Muslim world and beacon of light to the entire world. By glorifying Islam as taught and practised in Pakistan, these religious leaders are trying to delude the Muslim world. Perhaps it is their profession and a source of bread and butter that can never be called into question.

The new tax proposals have put an unrealistic burden on the industrial class. For example, the sugar and textile industry (major industries in West Pakistan) will be subject to capacity taxation whether that capacity is being fully utilized or not, and even if a mill or factory is closed, the owner has still to pay tax in proportion to its capacity. And if he fails to pay, the Government will confiscate his property. A very unrealistic and unimaginative proposal indeed. The impact will be felt in near future when due to falling production with no increase in wages, the prices of essential commodities will further go up almost breaking the back of a common man.

June 30

Once again, the people's hopes have been belied. The transfer of power to the elected representatives has been postponed for four months. When power is transferred, the new Government will function on the basis of a new constitution to be framed by a committee. Meanwhile the Awami League has been dubbed as an "open and armed rebellion against the state".

The dummies in state politics who could not win elections have come out with all praise for Yahya Khan. Maulana Maudoodi, founder of Jamaat-e-Islami, describes the President's speech for the proposed constitutional system as the most appropriate. Khan Abdul Qayuum Khan considers remedies provided very effective. Maulana Ghulam Ghaus Hazarvi, another leader, hails President's broadcast as "fulfilling aspirations of Pakistanis". Other leaders like Mian Tufail Mohammad and Nawabzada Nasurulla are all praise for the military regime and have welcomed the President's speech.

But Bhutto is silent. It could mean either a wave of unrest or his arrest.

July 3

Unemployment among the educated is on the rise. A local newspaper *Kohistan* reports that 50% of educated people are unemployed. 7,000 diploma holders in engineering, 1,500 graduate engineers and thousands of Masters of Science are unemployed. These numbers are registered with the Employment Exchanges. There are thousands who are not registered because in an employment exchange a person cannot get his name registered without bribing the officials, though registration does not automatically guarantee employment. No job is possible unless one has either the recommendation of a VIP or can grease the palm of the officials. The number of registered people in the Employment Exchanges in 1967 was nine lakh. It must have grown considerably by 1971 because of consistent lack of employment opportunities in every department, whether public or private.

For the job of one peon in a government office, 50% applications were from matriculates and 15% from intermediates. One 30-year old man committed suicide after 3 years of fruitless effort in getting a job. A young man says it is better to commit a crime because in the jail at least a person can get something to eat.

There were 3,500 applicants for just 15 posts in Accountant General's Office. There were 11,000 applicants for the posts of a few salesmen in a pharmaceutical firm. There may be hundreds whose application never reach their destination. Throughout Pakistan, the educated young are in a pitiable condition. They cannot get employment. They cannot ventilate their grievances in public because they are forbidden to take part in politics or express their views through the media. Out of frustration quite a few are turning to writing poetry, which gives them some mental satisfaction though it cannot fill their stomachs.

A lot of Pakistan currency is in the hands of Governments of Afghanistan, Saudi Arabia and Persian Gulf Countries. After demonetization, they are putting pressure on the Government of Pakistan to exchange it.

In many areas of Baluchistan, cut off from communications, many people are facing difficulties, as they could not deposit demonetized currency with the banks within the stipulated period. Articles of daily need there are hundred times more expensive than in Karachi. Most of the people, whose pride possessions are sheep and goats and mats made from palm trees, have virtually become paupers. Shopkeepers and people in general are so scared of further demonetizing of currency that they still do not accept even a fifty-rupee note, which is a valid tender.

Many medicines have disappeared from the market. In the city of Karachi alone 1,000 children are reported to be suffering from polio, but there is no medicine. Fifteen children have already died.

The economic figures released by the Government of Pakistan are as dubious as any other figures or data. With the exception of Baluchistan, which has shown a deficit of 7.22 crore Rupees, all other provinces have shown surplus budgets without raising additional taxes. The inside information tells a different story. It is reported that Punjab, NWFP and Baluchistan have increased their revenue by plugging leakages in the payment of local taxes and by raising taxes on items in the provincial list.

The arbitrary imposition of tax on personal incomes retrospectively from the year 1970-71 has created many problems particularly for the salaried people. It has also created problems for the business community. Appeals from all quarters are being made to the Government to revoke this order.

July 4

The Government has banned all private travel abroad except for business purposes. But on return every businessman will have to submit a report on the result of his visit abroad and in case of unsatisfactory result, he will be subject to penalties and likely to be blacklisted with the State Bank of Pakistan. That means he will not be able to go abroad again even though the purpose of his visit is genuine. Or else, he will have to wind up his business.

Trouble seems to be brewing in NWFP. Clashes are reported between landlords and tenants in Charade Tehsil (sub-Division of a District). More clashes are expected when the question of land leases and renewals of contracts between landlords and tenants comes up before the authorities this month. The landlords are so rich that they can easily bribe tehsidlars (land revenue collector in a Tehsil) and patwaries, who keep records of agricultural land, that they can get the revenue records changed in their favour.

In spite of recommendations made by the Taxation Commission appointed by the Government of Pakistan to impose tax on agricultural land, the provincial governments have not resorted to this harsh measure. It shows how powerful the landlord lobby is. Besides, large tracts of agricultural land are owned by corrupt Government officials and men in uniform.

The Government has refixed the quota of newsprint paper for printing and publishing of newspapers in the country.

July 5

The fear and panic in the minds of East Pakistanis cannot be easily removed in spite of protestations made by martial law authorities. Gradually an admission of the factual position in East Pakistan is coming out as borne by what retired Air Marshal Asghar Khan has to say, "The upheaval in this part of the country has left its scars on the minds and hearts of people which have to be sensibly and carefully removed". The people, he goes on to say, have to be resettled and confidence amongst them restored. He warns the next three months are likely to prove crucial for the future of Pakistan. He does not spell out why these months would be crucial. It could be the rainy season when the liberation forces in East Pakistan might have an upper hand over the Pakistani forces not too familiar with the terrain there or, it could be war with India.

The Pakistani press is sometimes also critical of Western powers particularly the United Kingdom. An editorial in the *Morning News* says "In the last three months the newspapers of the Western World appear to have devoted themselves to one objective, that is, to blacken the face of Pakistan by projecting the Indians as a nation of innocents. While the Indians are resorting to provocative military actions, can Pakistan for once hope to get a fair deal from the Western Press? Or, has the Western press given up objectivity and fair-mindedness merely because of a real or imaginary slight suffered by some correspondents (in Pakistan) three months ago?"

July 6

Every bureaucrat, every top brass in the armed forces and every politician in Pakistan knows that a common man, an average man, a poor and an illiterate man in Pakistan needs three things: bread, religion and diversion. Every effort is made to keep the prices of essential commodities like atta (wheat flour), oil, rice, soap, sugar and dalda (hydrogenated oil) under check. Every effort is made to make people rely more and more on Allah, who alone can bestow peace and prosperity and provide bread (forget butter). Lastly, every effort is made to divert people's attention by perpetually raising the bogey of India and by importing cheap sex films for feeding sex-hungry men. Those who can afford have more than one wife by law or otherwise and those who cannot afford satisfy their sexual urge by watching semi-nude western women in provocative poses and aimless and purposeless action in films of sex, suspense and adventure. That is how Pakistan keeps her people in good humour and hopes to survive on that. Whether it was Ayub Khan or it is Yahya Khan or whosoever comes next, the ploy is the same.

Mr. Bhutto has come out with a challenge to the Government, "—— by November, I will have either effective control or I will go to jail". Most probably he will go to jail because Yahya Khan is not going to transfer power to him and invite trouble for himself.

July 7

Pakistan out of sheer desperation born out of malice against India may choose war for revenge. The war will no doubt shatter her economy, but just to save her face among her people, the dictatorial Government may come out with the plea of 'inevitability'. The Government is finding it extremely difficult to run the country with limited economic resources.

Sushil Chandra, a colleague of mine and I live in a big house designed for an officer of the level of Director in the Ministry. It was built in those days when the capital of Pakistan had not shifted from Karachi to Islamabad. As it has been lying vacant, it was allotted to us. Both of us are here without our families. The house is too big for us. But we have got to maintain and manage it. Though the house is furnished, we have limited kitchen utensils. As we do not know when we may have to pack up, we are wary of adding to our meager possessions. A Bengali Muslim servant, who used to cook for us, has been fired. He was too lazy, a sort of vagabond and disobedient. A class-four servant, the rank of a peon, cooks for us these days. The food is as insipid as our existence and stay. We cannot mix freely with the local people. We cannot invite anybody and nobody would invite us. There is not much to see in Karachi and the Pakistan Foreign Office does not permit us to go outside Karachi. That is our life here. Money cannot always buy peace of mind and a comfortable living. I am more or less reconciled to the situation. I take it that if I were lucky, separated from my family for an indefinite or imprecise period, I would not have come here.

July 8

Some people in Pakistan still live in a fool's paradise. One Mian Amir-ud-Din thinks India should concede territory upto Agra on western side and Bihar on eastern side to rehabilitate Muslims of India who have no security. He imagines that the Muslims in India are starving, while those in Pakistan have their stomachs full. Fundamentalism obscures judgement and places faith in Jihad (holy war against the infidels – all non-Muslims, with the avowed object of annihilating them from the surface of the earth or converting them to Islam) that the Muslims think will ensure a safe and lasting place in paradise.

July 10

The means of transportation and communication in East Pakistan are still disrupted. Workers are still afraid of coming to work. The poor helpless Government officials, teachers, policemen, and railway workers, all low paid job holders in West Pakistan are being forced to go to East Pakistan to work there. Those who have a clout with the high Government officials can manage to wriggle out, but the rest, who are in majority, have to go there willy-nilly to face death and the wrath of the Bengalis.

To Pakistan which has not seen a free press for all these years, any criticism directed against her, whether within the country or outside, comes as a rude shock. There is no self analysis, no soul searching. Anybody, howsoever genuinely concerned and well intentioned, who criticizes Pakistan, is dubbed as enemy of Pakistan. These days the countries of Western Europe, USA and Canada are dubbed by the media as enemies of Pakistan because they have not supported Pakistan for her ruthless actions in East Pakistan.

We are still without a servant. It is difficult to get a local servant. Most of them are afraid of working with us because of the presence and questioning by Pakistan intelligence men posted outside the Chancery building and our residences. Most of the shopkeepers from whom we buy groceries, fruits and vegetables, the barber, the laundryman and the baker, all know that we are from the Indian High Commission, but other than the business of selling they do not utter a single extra word and even wish us. They dread the consequences of talking politics or for that matter an any other matter with us. It is not that they are ignorant. They know what is happening between India and Pakistan, but they would not like to talk about it. Still it goes to their credit that they also do not show any hostility or talk in a curt and impolite language. They talk business in a businesslike fashion without a smile and without a welcome nod.

July 11

Pakistan's attitude towards China is one of hero-worship. China is a model, a beacon of light, and an ideal for every economic, social and political ill of Pakistan. China is a model for agricultural reforms. China is a model for political reforms. China is a model for type of education in schools, colleges and universities. China is a model for sacrifices, which every Pakistani must make for the peace and prosperity of the country. China is being eulogized with the twin object of pleasing her and telling the common man in Pakistan that Pakistan is not without friends, although the USA, the UK, and other Western countries and even the Arab world has not given any meaningful help to Pakistan in her hour of need.

This kind of hero-worship equally suits China because in Pakistan she has found a reliable needy ally to be the common enemy of India. People are made to believe that China is Pakistan's best friend, while others like the USA, the Western Countries and even the Arab Countries are fair weather friends.

Colleges and universities have become centers of corruption. Girls are being abducted both by the students and the outsiders. Two girls were abducted from Garden College, Rawalpindi by four students, one of whom was a relative of Sardar Shukat Hyat, a political leader, and the other three were workers of the Muslim League (Qayyum Group). The Principal of Sahiwal Girls College for many years had been withdrawing money from college funds for her personal use with the overt connivance of the authorities. She is keeping them happy by supplying girls and feels no shame as a woman in exploiting the weakness of her own sex.

Mrs. Khan, the principal of Abdul Sttar Government College Sahiwal, also used college money for her personal needs. Over and above she extracted money, in kind or cash, from her staff. The story goes that when her driver demanded money for the vegetables he bought for her from the market, she dismissed him from service.

There is an open flesh trade in private hostels. One girl tells the story of being sold to different men. Another girl was blackmailed by replacing the face of a naked girl in a photograph with that of hers. Nobody would believe her story that she was innocent.

The Daily *Hurriat* and the *Jang* every day report cases of murder, abduction and rape. Most of the offenders are never caught because they have the backing of influential and wealthy people.

Many factories are lying idle for want of raw materials and capital coupled with fall in demand. In many factories there are no labour laws or regulations to protect the rights of workers. They are not allowed to form unions and can be hired and fired any time at the sweet will of the management, without even a formal notice.

The Stock Exchanges are daily showing bearish tendencies. Various trade organizations are sending memoranda to the Government on account of hardships faced by the industry caused by the new budgetary proposals that contain repressive tax measures.

The farmers are trying their best to resist imposition of agricultural tax. The price of sugarcane and cotton has gone down because of refusal by mills to lift the stocks. They were sending most of these finished products to East Bengal. Due to the turmoil there, the movement of all goods from West to East has stopped. The purchasing power of the common man in West Pakistan has been eroded through demonetization of currency.

July 14

Today's *Hurriat* reports that the trial, which is not open to the public, of Sheikh Mujib-ur-Rahman and his constitutional adviser Dr. Kamal Hussain on charges of treason, setting up a parallel government, inciting the masses to commit murders and sabotage and conspiring against the Government of Pakistan, has begun.

Out of 169 MLAs in East Pakistan, the election of about 100 has been held illegal by the Government of Pakistan. Obviously they were the staunch supporters of Mujib. The by-elections will be held in the first week of October.

The earlier decision of the Government to nationalize banks has been kept in abeyance. The explanation is that the Government does not have experienced bankers and nationalization may consequently lead to a chaos in financial circles.

Many countries like the UK, Japan and the USA are refusing to honour letters of credit opened by Pakistani banks. Even China is not making full supplies though accepting the letters of credit. China is keeping a close watch on the economy of Pakistan.

The Government does not intend to print currency notes of higher denomination. New currency notes of hundred and fifty rupees denomination may be issued, but it is uncertain when that may be the case.

The Government of Pakistan is reported to have forced sugar mills to export 12.5 lakh sacks of sugar, each weighing 2.75 maunds (roughly 250 kg) to Kuwait and the Persian Gulf countries to earn much needed foreign exchange. The export price is less than 50 to 60% of domestic price. It is for this reason the procurement price of sugarcane was reduced some time ago causing hardship to sugarcane growers.

July 17

President Nixon's acceptance of invitation from Chou En-lai to visit China is being hailed by Pakistani press and radio as Pakistan's victory, especially Yahya Khan's diplomacy. Much is being made of the fact that Dr. Kissinger had slipped secretly into China from Pakistan during his Asian tour from July 9 to July 11. It is considered to be a matter of pride for Pakistan that Yahya Khan alone knew of the secret. Pakistan is simultaneously projecting the idea that India is unhappy over this development despite the fact that India had been trying much earlier for the admission of China into UNO.

Pakistan is trying to export as much as possible to earn foreign exchange. Large quantities of cement have been exported to Persian Gulf countries. To arrest use of cement at home, the construction of new buildings was banned in the new budget announced earlier.

Pakistan will cease every opportunity to excite Muslims in India. Any clash between the Hindus and the Muslims in India is prominently reported by the media giving it a wide coverage.

Pakistan also makes it a point to spotlight the grievances of the Bengalis in West Bengal, protests made by the Sikhs against interference by the Indian Government in their internal affairs and other political events of that kind to tell her people that India is no better than Pakistan.

Commenting on the national dress prescribed by the President of Azad Kashmir a student says that while lakhs of people in Pakistan cannot get cloth to cover their bodies, how a particular dress can forge unity among the people.

One Parsee has been refused foreign exchange facilities for pilgrimage to India. When he drew the attention of the officer to the release of foreign exchange to the Muslims for purposes of pilgrimage, the officer told him curtly that the facility was meant for Muslims only. The paradoxical thing is that Pakistan claims that the state gives equal treatment to all communities irrespective of caste and creed.

One woman living in a place known as Nusrat relates a horrible tale of incest committed by a father on his daughter and later on divorcing the mother and living together with his daughter with their new born baby. This happened when the mother went to her parents' house leaving behind the young daughter to look after her father.

July 18

Inconsistency presumably born out of frustration is the hallmark of Pakistan's foreign policy. The same newspapers, which once abused the USA, are now praising that country on the eve of the arrival of Henry Kissinger. Pakistan is hoping to see a solution to her economic ills in the USA-China dialogue on reconciliation. But Chinese intentions can never be clear. The day China extended an invitation to President Nixon, Chinese armed forces chief Huang Yung Sheng accused the USA of planning aggression against China.

Pakistan thinks she has played a decisive role in arranging a meeting between Chou and Nixon. Even though the US State Department spokesman Charles Bray has declined comment on the arrangements made by Pakistan, yet Pakistan is indulging in self-praise and wishful thinking. She considers it a great diplomatic victory that will further strengthen her bonds both with the USA and China and inversely, damage the relations between India and the USA.

July 19

Pakistan is much worried about her jute industry in East Pakistan. If she cannot meet world demand this season, substitutes are likely to pose threat to the jute industry which is the largest export earner for Pakistan. But the jute industry in East Pakistan is totally paralyzed. Stupendous efforts will be required for rehabilitation. Jute exports hitherto have been bringing maximum foreign exchange for Pakistan. No doubt, the Government is much concerned with the loss of much-sought after foreign exchange.

The student community in general does not seem to indulge in anti-India propaganda or malign India as their elders do. Perhaps they understand the game plan of the Military rulers or they understand the significance of democracy or both. They do not seem to buy the explanations given by their rulers that the democracy is unsuited for Pakistan and that the Military Rule is the best solution for the welfare of Pakistan They have a clear perception that the military rulers want to occupy their chairs by hook or by crook. One often hears or reads criticism on the manner in which the economy of Pakistan is being tackled and the problems of education and unemployment are being tackled, but one seldom hears a student speaking against India. Presumably the demonstrations led by the students denouncing India's interference in East Pakistan have been tutored and there are many outsiders among them.

Dates! It is for the first time after I migrated to India in 1947 that I had a relish of green juicy delicious dates coming direct from the trees of Multan, Muzaffargarh, Bahawlapur and Jhung. One has to taste the dates from these areas to appreciate the delicacy of the fruit.

July 21

A deliberate and conscious effort has been set afoot through newspapers, radio and television to generate anti-India hysteria. In television programmes like DEKH KABIRA ROYA and PLATFORM, Hindus are depicted as mean fellows and Hindu gods and goddesses and India's leaders are brazenly caricatured and blatantly ridiculed. Hindu customs, traditions and culture are not only mocked at but also viciously abused.

A poet like Hafiz Jallundhri, who migrated from India, has compared India to a she-demon. He says that even though India is a land of gods and goddesses, they all have Muslim blood by which he means Hindu women having illicit relations with Muslim men. He provokes the people of Pakistan to get ready to fight against India because Muslims are not safe there. He seems to be trying to step into the shoes of Urdu poet Iqbal, who died some time back and was known for championing the cause of Indian Muslims by joining hands with other Muslim leaders in erstwhile undivided India in demanding a separate homeland for the Muslims that he named Pakistan.

In the serial PLATFORM scenes of 1947 partition are being simulated to impress and educate the young generations how and at what cost Pakistan was achieved. A map of partitioned India is set on fire. While the entire India burns, through the grace of God, only that portion called Pakistan remains unburnt. This is also intended to confuse the people of Pakistan that Bangladesh is a creation of India and that India is bent upon disintegrating Pakistan.

The announcement of Chou-Nixon meeting in May 1971 has further encouraged Pakistan to adopt aggressive posture against India. Pakistan is assuming that if she has a war against India, the USA, under the influence of China through her newly formed friendship, will not support India and point out an accusing finger towards Pakistan. Pakistan is straining every nerve to hold East Pakistan, which is gradually slipping from her fingers.

July 22

Pakistan trade statistics do not show export of jute during the last three months, but newspapers mention export of jute worth six crore rupees. Who is exporting is a mystery.

Every effort is being made to merge the three factions of Muslim League into one to set against Bhutto's Pakistan Peoples Party. The idea is to keep Bhutto away from the centre of power.

Pakistan has further stepped up anti-India propaganda with the object of fomenting the Hindu-Muslim riots. She has two ostensible objects. One is to reduce the impact of Awami League in India and the other is to drown Bangladesh issue in Hindu-Muslim riots. It is also expected that in the event of riots in India, most of the Muslims will migrate to East Pakistan thereby reducing the Bengalis to a minority. What wishful thinking!

Pakistan has not given any details of 65 Bengali personnel working in the Pakistan High Commission in Calcutta. Only a passing reference has been made that they were interviewed by the Swiss representative in the presence of Pakistani official Mehdui Masud.

One Salim Gillani is writing parodies on the songs sung by Indian singer Lata Mangeshkar. These are sung by a Pakistani singer Shanaz Gul. Some of the parodies are:

Gangaram ke samajh mein na aye (Gangaram does not understand)

Aye Sharnarthi jana na (O refugee, don't leave me)

Mein hun ek bhikari (I am a beggar)

Gidar bhabki kuin dete ho? (Why do you give me empty threats?

Mera Sundar sapna toot gaya (My sweet dream ended abruptly?}

July 25,

Blacking out of all news from East Pakistan detrimental to the interest of Pakistan is no tribute to the freedom of the press. In fact eulogizing and paying handsome tributes to the man in power is the weakness of the press. Any attempt to pierce the thick pall of censorship means torture and imprisonment. Whosoever has tried to raise a finger against the Government has been severely dealt with. When Ayub Khan was in power the press lifted him to the skies but soon after his downfall the same press condemned him. Perhaps the same fate awaits Yahya Khan.

July 27

The English newspapers give only selected news suitable for the foreigners. But Urdu newspapers give detailed news and surprisingly conflicting versions or opposite views of happenings in both the wings of Pakistan.

Mr. S.B. Zaman, an elected representative of Awami League is on a visit to Karachi. In a Press Conference he said that he still stuck to six-point programme. He added he had talks with Bhutto who accepted five out of six programmes, but he hoped Bhutto would accept the 6th programme too. But he made it clear that he wanted to implement the six-point programme within the Yaha Khan's constitutional framework. He has invited Bhutto to East Pakistan and hopes that Bhutto will get support from the Awami League. He thinks Muslim League, which is responsible for the present situation in the country, is dead. Its politics is confined to the drawing room. He has suggested that action should be taken against Bhashani, Atta-ul-Rahman and Prof. Muzaffar – all members of the Muslim League, who in collusion with the anti-state elements, Naxalites and secessionists, hatched a conspiracy against Pakistan.

Some secret papers from the personal file of Qaid-e-Azam Jinah are reported to have been stolen by one Fazal-ul-Alam, who has since fled to England. Of course, this has been denied by the Government.

Bhutto is being strongly criticised for his interview with a Tehran daily, particularly his assertion that he seeks a settlement with India and the Awami League in East Pakistan. He has emphasized the need for the participation of duly elected members of the Awami League in shaping the future settlement by framing a new constitution and establishing up a democratic Government in Pakistan. He has accused the army of making a fatal mistake in killing innocent people in East Pakistan. He has denied that these killings were the handiwork of Indian agents- provocateurs. The criticism has come mainly from the elite Punjabi element, which has never liked Bhutto, a Sindhi, even though his party won the elections.

July 28

After Nixon's acceptance of invitation from Peking, Pakistan feels emboldened and from a defensive posture hitherto she is moving towards an aggressive posture against India.

Pakistani writers (mostly of poor standing) are spending their energies on writing cheap type of satires full of abuse and vulgarity against India. Everything Indian - Indian culture, Indian religion (mainly Hinduism), Indian leaders, Indian democracy - all are attacked indiscriminately without any sense of decency. In this way these unknown writers not only make some money for a living, but also get into limelight. It is not surprising that so much space is devoted to anti-India propaganda that nothing is left for any sensible writing and for any work of art and literature.

The writers of some caliber (though very few) are keeping a low profile. Unless India is openly ridiculed and maligned, nothing else will get printed or shown on the television. It may be all right from Yahya Khan's angle to malign India, but this way Pakistan is suffocating the growth of its culture and literature. It is commonly known that one cannot get good books on art, culture and literature in Pakistan, because no effort has been made to encourage fine arts. A few Muslim writers and thinkers of some merit who migrated from India at the time of partition are in a miserable condition. Their conscience perhaps does not allow them to write anything unethical and untrue, but they cannot see their names in print and make a living unless they write something against India, howsoever untrue and vulgar. No wonder some have fallen prey to the needs of the body and have started using their pens against India.

Bhutto is trying his best to arrive at a practical compromise with the elected representatives of the Awami League, whereas Yahya Khan and his proteges are trying to resuscitate Muslim League. Whether the Muslim League reemerges as a single party in Pakistan or not, Bhutto is least likely to have a taste of power for which he is clamouring and crying hoarse.

July 29

Will Pakistan quit the Commonwealth and break off diplomatic relations with India? It is strongly rumoured that she may do both though not necessarily at the same time. She may quit Commonwealth because the U.K. has completely exposed her on Bangladesh issue. She may break off diplomatic relations with India, necessitated perhaps by the defection of 65 Bengalis manning the Pakistan Deputy High Commission in Calcutta and blaming India for the debacle in East Pakistan.

All efforts are being made by the Jamat-e-Islami and the Muslim League to see that Bhutto's Pakistan Peoples Party does not come into power by having a political settlement with the Awami League. Every political party, small or big, seems to be living in a fool's paradise because Yahya Khan as President of Pakistan is most unlikely to quit his office. Lack of understanding and cooperation among various political parties suits the agenda of Yahya Khan.

July 30

I saw a man sitting on a pavement listening to an Indian film song from a transistor lying nearby. It makes no difference to him if the song is from an Indian film or a Pakistani film so long as he understands the language of that sad song. I have heard Indian music being played on marriages, in restaurants, in taxis and perhaps in the bedrooms of affluent people. Music knows no barriers. If it is a rich man's entertainment, it is a poor man's solace. By listening to sad music a poor man is perhaps trying to drown his sorrows that have no end for him.

Once I read a letter to the Editor of *Morning News* from a Pakistani that All India Radio announced fictitious names that make requests for playing their favourite film songs on air. But judging from the popularity of Indian film songs in Pakistan I can say with a certain degree of certainty that these names are not fictitious. Most of the Pakistani films are copies of Indian films.

July 31

The fees in Government schools in Karachi have been increased. The Education Board says that this step was necessary because of drastic cut in aid from the Government. The management has appealed to the parents to cooperate with the schools otherwise closure would be the only alternative.

August 1

A picnic to Hawks Bay was quite enjoyable, if not thrilling because the sea was rough making it difficult to swim or even stand in the waters disturbed by the roaring waves that struck the coastline with the ferocity of a storm. The sky was intermittently cloudy and whenever the sun came out, it was very sharp. Nevertheless, this is the best beach in Karachi.

When we returned at 5.40 p.m. we found about 50 policemen standing in front of our Chancery building. They had been there for about half an hour. We were alarmed. But our anxiety ended when we learnt that the police had been called for security arrangements for the President who was going to have dinner with the erstwhile Nawab of Junagarh who lived in a palatial building across the road right in front of our Chancery building.

August 4

For a long time Pakistan had been trying to conceal from her people that atrocities were in fact committed by her armed forces in East Bengal, but it was not possible to hide the truth for all times. Now she has come forward with a strange argument that what Pakistan had done in East Pakistan, India did exactly the same in Nagaland and Kashmir. In fact, the people living in West Pakistan have not shed any tears on the killings of Bengalis in East Pakistan. They argue that as Bengalis including Hindus living in East Pakistan slaughtered non-Bengalis, the army had to act sternly to save the country from disintegration.

The position of employed women in Pakistan is very pathetic. Nurses are objects of lust for the doctors, private secretaries for their bosses, teachers for the management, and like that there are many tales of lust and exploitation of the weaker sex. Special care is taken to recruit beautiful girls irrespective of their educational qualifications. The real merit is beauty and after that consent.

One school got Government grant and recognition and later on good report because the Principal and all the teachers were beautiful and they compromised with the inspectors and the management.

One patient in a hospital had to die because he objected to the doctor's advances towards his sister, a student of nursing class. The doctor neglected him.

The bosses in commercial firms consider women employees as their second wives. One commercial manager of Pakistan Radio got an employee girl abducted and raped because she spurned his advances.

One nurse working in a hospital says that the doctors, the lab assistants, the nurses, and the jamadars (cleaners and garbage collectors) take care of only those patients who grease their palms. Poor patients are treated like street curs.

Yahya Khan's televised interviews with the correspondents from the U.S.A., the U.K., Japan and Canada showed that irrespective of the questions put to him, his replies were stereotyped and evasive. How poor his vocabulary is can be judged from the use of words and the phrases like "jolt from the blue", "genociding", "I am unbalanced", and many more.

August 6

The White Paper on East Pakistan released by the Government is full of patent lies and fabrications and inconsistencies. It will not be possible for Pakistan to justify the events after the army took action and after the expulsions of foreign correspondents from East Pakistan. This nation does not seem to have a common guilt conscience. The people at the helm of affairs in the Pakistan bureaucracy, in the armed forces and pathetically in the media, all without exception tell patent lies and on the face of it proclaim themselves as the most truthful people in the world.

August 8

It is reported that in Afghanistan a campaign is being carried out in favour of Bangladesh. Even some clashes have taken place between the pro-Bangladeshi and the pro-Pakistanis.

A demand is being made to issue another White Paper on the economic viability of East Pakistan. It is being argued that East Pakistan could not be developed as fast as West Pakistan because for centuries its economy was dominated by the Hindu banyas (merchant class). Even after partition, the economy of East Pakistan, as alleged by the Government of Pakistan, has been controlled by the Hindus who have illegally transferred money to India. It is another face saving device by apportioning the blame to India.

The politics of Pakistan is a strange phenomenon. On the one hand the Awami League has been banned and on the other hand 88 seats have been declared null and void, giving an opportunity to the remaining elected representatives to revolt against the party in order to create a rift within the party.

The Jan Sangh demonstration on the 7th in front of Pakistan High Commission in New Delhi has been prominently reported by the local newspapers. If there are no protest rallies and demonstrations in Pakistan, what could be the reason? There could be two reasons: first, if the Government allows such gatherings, the people may start protesting against their own Government for all the wrongs done, and secondly, the Government does not have enough police force to control the mobs, if they become unruly. A large chunk of police force has been sent to East Pakistan.

August 12

In this country income earned by the schools and the colleges through grants and donations is misappropriated for political ends. It is reported that the Islamic institutions make twenty lakh rupees every year through dishonest means. It is, therefore, not surprising that education of boys and girls is woefully neglected.

A strong speculation is afloat that Mujib-ur-Rahman may be hanged. It is to be seen if Yahya Khan will yield to the pressure of world powers to spare his life.

The signing of Indo-Soviet treaty has caused ripples and dismay in political circles in Pakistan. The bellicose attitude adopted by Pakistan against India has suddenly been toned down. The Military regime is struggling to have a matching partner – the

United States of America or China. With which country Pakistan will enter into an alliance is an open question. It is unlikely any of the two will oblige Pakistan to have a sort of treaty on the lines of the Indo-Soviet treaty.

The members of National Assembly-elect on the Awami League ticket are afraid of coming out of their hideouts in East Pakistan.

August 14

Without giving up their anti-India stance the newspapers, on the eve of the Pakistan Independence Day, have come out with self-criticism and heart-searching. "Every Pakistani today should shed the veneer of emotionalism, divest himself of hypocrisy and give up pretending. It is because of our emotionalism, hypocrisy and pretensions that we find ourselves propelled to the brink of disaster", says one daily newspaper. In Pakistan "Everything was done in the name of the people, but the will of the poor people never came into play", says another newspaper. Though independence of India and creation of Pakistan came on the same day, that is, 15 August 1947, Pakistan chose to celebrate her Independence Day a day before, that is, 14 August so as not to coincide with India's Independence Day (August 15) for reasons that were not spelled out by the then newly formed Government of Pakistan.

Pakistan is ostensibly disturbed over the Indo-Soviet treaty of "peace, friendship and cooperation". She cannot afford to antagonize Russia because of her mighty power. Pakistan is finding fault with her foreign policy and more so with her diplomats abroad for failing to project the right image of Pakistan. But Pakistan does not realize that the diplomats will do what they are told to do by their bosses at home. In one's own country it is easy to befool the poor and illiterate masses, but in a foreign land where the media is independent, it is not possible to dictate terms and censor foreign news.

As expected General Tikka Khan has been awarded Hilal-I-Quaid-I-Azam, the highest military award. One is, however, surprised to see a long list of persons who have been given awards on the eve of the Pakistan Independence Day. Most of them were even unheard and thus least deserving.

The results of Matriculation examinations have been postponed for four days because of shortage of newsprint. It can happen in a country like Pakistan where education has the least priority. In fact, historically, Muslims have been the most uneducated people in the world. It may be religiously feasible to lay emphasis on the teachings of Quran, but without imparting the scientific knowledge no country can, in the modern world, survive economically at least. Unfortunately, the people, who handle the national affairs, are least educated to understand the value of education.

August 15

We had a brief flag hoisting ceremony for our Independence Day on the premises of the Chancery building. There was light refreshment served at the expense of the India Club, which collects contributions from all the officials. The representational officers (above the rank of an Attachι, the lowest diplomatic officer) have in the present circumstances rare occasions to throw parties to the Pakistanis, who would think ten times before accepting an invitation. But they keep on drawing the monthly representational grant sanctioned by the Government of India. They could have easily spent some of the grant on refreshments instead of drawing from the India Club.

A student in a televised programme said that half of the Quran was full of superstitions and was diametrically opposed to reasoning and logic. In another televised programme a few days ago a student said that in schools and colleges the wrong type of history of Pakistan was being taught. The students get disillusioned with the history by Pakistani authors, when they read books written by famous world historians.

Pakistan had painted such a rosy picture of her success in 1965 war with India that every student had come to believe that Pakistan was victorious and it was a grave mistake on the part of Ayub Khan to have signed Tashkent Agreement. But Ayub Khan had this to say, "We could not win Kashmir on the battlefront, how we could do that on the conference table? We wanted an opening". Even the Pakistani correspondents who had covered the Tashkent talks insisted that the best they could achieve had been achieved. (Lengthening Shadows by S. Shabir Hussain). Some of the prominent leaders like Bhashani, Nurul Amin, Farid Ahmed and Arif Aftikhar welcomed the agreement. But it can be said the people in general and the student community in particular got angry. Why? The entire nation was fed on blatant lies. They were promised hoisting of the Pakistan flag on the Red Fort in Delhi and liberation of India occupied Kashmir. It was difficult to give any logical explanation for the abrupt signing of the Tashkent Agreement in which most of the Pakistanis saw Pakistan conceding defeat.

Ayub Khan had to pay the price, whereas Bhutto, who was equally responsible for the 1965 debacle, escaped any censure because of his cleverness and cunningness. The moment he realized that continuing with 1965 war hysteria would mean his downfall, he quietly left the stage. It is strange that the student community still considers Bhutto a hero of the 1965 war and a leader of the masses.

Money is not everything in life. We cannot get what we may like to get because of so many restrictions on our movements. It is a sort of solitary confinement. We crave for the free air.

August 16

Many political leaders like Maudoodi and Qayyum feel that the existence of Pakistan is in danger. Even newspaper editorials and articles are saying the same thing. It is being openly projected that Pakistan was created on Islamic ideology in the fervent hope that the Muslims would be able to lead a life of their own based on tenets of Islam. But all their hopes and aspirations have remained unfulfilled. On the contrary doubts are being expressed about the unity and national solidarity of Pakistan. In this country created by a special will of God as the fundamentalists proclaim with the beat of a drum, without shedding any blood, without waging a war and without compromising self-respect, why nepotism, self-aggrandizement, favoritism, selfishness, dishonesty, bribery and personal glory have become the trademark of Pakistan's political and social system. That is the question the masses in Pakistan ask. The trouble is nobody has the courage to condemn Yahya Khan or hold him responsible for adopting draconian measures in East Pakistan that have not only shattered the economy, the political and social life of average Pakistani, but have also made him pessimistic on the future of Pakistan.

It is a pity that instead of putting her own house in order Pakistan is all the time accusing outside powers, in particular India, of interfering in her internal affairs. Some writers have now mustered the courage to say, correctly, that Pakistan is labouring under a wrong impression that she can never be divided because of Islamic ideology. The situation particularly in East Pakistan has gone out of control and mammoth efforts will be required to keep Pakistan united or only a miracle can save Pakistan from disintegration.

Yahya Khan has certainly lost his mental poise. He becomes vociferous at everything that does not agree with his temperament.

August 17

Any mention of India by anyone in a conciliatory tone, not to speak of a friendly tone, is considered a crime against Islam. The whole strategy of the Government of Pakistan these days is to feed her own people with wrong ideas principally directed against India. By reviving the memories of pre-partition and partition days, Pakistan is trying to build a new Pakistan to cover up her crimes of brutality and butchery in East Pakistan.

August 20

Some people have come out with a fantastic theory that the Government of India wanted to get Mujib-ur-Rehman kidnapped from West Pakistan and for this purpose the Indian High Commissioner in Islamabad was instructed to find out the ways and means of achieving the end. They further say that the High Commissioner told the Government of India that as the Sheikh was heavily guarded, it was not possible to get him kidnapped. It is only after the High Commissioner expressed his inability, so it is alleged, did the Prime Minister of India sent messages to the Secretary General of the UNO and other world leaders to save the life of Mujib-ur-Rehman

Pakistan had started making war-like preparations after being emboldened by Nixon's acceptance of an invitation from China. But India's treaty of friendship with Russia has dampened her spirits to some extent. Pakistan has now sent her Foreign Secretary Mr. S.M. Khan to Moscow to get an assurance from Kremlin that in the event of war with India the treaty will not be used against Pakistan. If Russia gives that kind of assurance, which is very doubtful, Pakistan will revert to the old game of playing her cards against India with greater confidence.

August 22

Anti-Hindu propaganda directed against the Hindus in Sind has been stepped up. There are not many Hindus in other provinces of West Pakistan. Short of branding them as traitors, it is alleged that these Hindus move about in suspicious circumstances (by implication spying for India) and carry on their business covertly.

Many textile mills have been closed because of increase in the price of raw cotton without a corresponding increase in the price of cloth. The increase in price is due to shortage of cotton in the domestic market. A large quantity has been exported to earn the fast depleting foreign exchange. There is also no demand for cloth in East Pakistan due to disturbed conditions.

The incidence of crime in Karachi is on the increase. Parents are afraid of sending their daughters to schools. Cases of murder, rape and kidnapping have multiplied.

The sale of wheat flour (atta) is subsidized in Karachi by the provincial Government of Sind. It is reported that every year the Government undergoes a loss of one crore rupees by providing wheat to the mills at reduced rates. But this concession does not pass to the actual consumers. The flour mills take out high percentage of maida (cream of whole wheat) and then mix the residue with inferior quality grain.

It is for the first time that a newspaper has given the story of the defection of Mr Hasan Ali, the former Pakistan Deputy High Commissioner in Calcutta. Mention has also been made of an official who defected from Pakistan Embassy in Switzerland and the disappearance of one Fazal Mohammed, who took away with him papers relating to Quaid-e-Azam from Islamabad.

August 24

Pakistan's hatred against India knows no limits. In a dispatch from London, *Pakistan Times*' correspondent uses mean and ugly words against Ajit Wadekear, the captain of the Indian Cricket team, when commenting on the match between India and Pakistan being played at Oval. Though India won the match, the Pakistan media has no word of praise for the Indian team.

Kaneez Fatima, a labour leader, has said that industrial establishments have retrenched fifty percent workers. The Pakistan Peoples' Party which won elections for the cause of the labour class has done nothing to raise a voice against the mill owners.

I have no doubt that most of the affluent Muslims in India have one foot in India and they try to keep another foot in Pakistan. They want to have the best of both the worlds. Even the daughter of Nawab of Chhatari was married to a Punjabi physician of Pakistan in 1964. She eventually migrated to Pakistan in 1965. She visits India almost every year.

Bhutto is still clamouring for transfer of power. He is likely to go wild and that is exactly what the Government wants so that they can hook him up.

August 28

The blackout exercises yesterday, though a success, were not without blemishes. There was an element of rowdyism. Street urchins and miscreants threw stones at buildings and broke windowpanes. They punctured the tyres of public vehicles on the road and manhandled ladies seated in cars. They teased girls and looted some shops. The local newspapers have criticized the ugly events.

The newspapers report that 4,000 workers have become jobless on account of retrenchment in textile mills. The unofficial figure is much more. All the textile mills are virtually running into loss. No goods can be sold in East Pakistan and the purchasing power of the people in West Pakistan has been eroded due to inflation and much loss of business activity and ban on construction of new buildings thus reducing the earnings per capita. Many days ago the Government announced compensation upto rupees one lakh per person for the demonetized currency, but not a single payment has been made so far and no payment is likely to be made as the exchequer has run short of funds due to costly operations in East Pakistan.

August 29

Since the day the Pakistan's Independence Day was celebrated on August 14, articles and write-ups have appeared in newspapers and many Urdu magazines in which the people of Pakistan through the writers have expressed their profound sorrow that after so many years of independence, Pakistan is still not mentally free. A separate homeland was demanded for Muslims on the premise that they would be able to lead a life of their own in accordance with the tenets of Islam, but there is so much of corruption, nepotism and favouritism that nobody can breathe freely. Unless one is rich or a big shot to have a clout with the Military Rulers and the bureaucrats in the Government, an average man faces many obstacles in his daily life.

It is reported that some troop movement has started on the Western Front with India. Pakistan has raised two more divisions during the last 3 or 4 months. She has lost one division in East Pakistan. There are in all four divisions in East Pakistan of which three are deployed on the western border with India.

An interesting controversy has arisen whether the late Prime Minister of Pakistan, Mr Liaquat Ali Khan, was a victim of conspiracy or his murder was an act of madness by an individual. No conclusion is possible.

West Pakistanis have a sort of hatred for the Bengalis from East Pakistan working in West Pakistan. Mujib-ul-Rehman Khan, Head of the Bengali Language Department in Islamia College, Karachi has been charged with the act of composing 'Joy Bangla' – a song eulogizing the Bengalis, and removed from his post. It is reported that many Bengalis have been removed from key posts in West Pakistan.

Pakistan is under heavy firing from her own people living abroad for giving concocted versions of happenings in both the wings of Pakistan. As a matter of fact Pakistanis working for their Government in foreign lands are in a delicate position. Should they back up the wrong policies of their Government or should they speak the truth? The information and relevant data that they get from the foreign media, in sharp contrast to the feeds they get from their own Government, gives them a true picture of their own country.

August 31

Sometimes I wonder what the people of Pakistan think and how they feel what is happening around them. Pakistan was supposed to be a paradise as vociferously and confidently proclaimed by their leaders in undivided India, but in reality it has become a hell for the masses. They have no voice. They have no rights. They cannot expect justice and fair play. They are like dumb driven cattle blindly following the voice of their shepherd.

I can hear the shouts of children playing across the wall on my right. I hear the noises coming from the apartments facing our house. But nobody looks towards us as if we are outcasts living in a forbidden land. Many of us were once one before partition divided us. We did not separate like brothers but rather like enemies and the feeling of animosity that should have died with the passage of time lingers on and these days it has suddenly erupted like a volcano lying dormant for some time.

I had an attack of malaria that confined me to bed for three days. I am grateful to Sushil Chandra, my roommate, for looking after me. But when he was gone to office, I felt lonely. I had to struggle to get a glass of water or go to the toilet. Of course, I feel much better and should be back on my agile feet in a day or two. Lying in the bed, I have reflections on the past: what I was when I began life and how I had to struggle without any encouragement and assistance from any quarter, to stand on my own feet. Then comes the thought of tomorrow that seems so far off and when it comes, it passes so quickly merging in the vastness of the past. The vacuum of loneliness seldom gets filled to the brim. There is never ending thought of tomorrow teaming with false hopes of a lasting happiness. Despite knowing the realities of life, we still live in dreams – in a make-believe world. But philosophically speaking, it is the dreams of tomorrow that sustain life to today.

September 1

The appointment of Dr. Abdul Motaleb Malik as Governor of East Pakistan, expected for the last one week, has not come as a surprise. He was born in Kushtia district of East Pakistan in 1905. He is a Special Assistant to the President for East Pakistan affairs. His appointment is viewed in political circles as a first step towards restoration of democracy in East Pakistan because he is a civilian. He is pro-Western, but it is doubtful if he will have an effective control and will be able to restore normalcy and democracy in East Pakistan. It is also doubtful if the people of East Pakistan will accept him. The Mukti Bahini will surely not allow him to rest in peace. The move is perhaps too late.

Another appointment of Lt. Gen. Niazi as Martial Law Administrator in East Pakistan in place of Lt. Gen. Tikka Khan has come as a surprise. The surprising part is that Tikka Khan is stated to have done a wonderful job in East Pakistan. Either he has done his job too harshly or he is a contender for power. The game is being played by General Hamid. Once again it is proved beyond doubt that the Punjabi element has an upper hand in controlling the destiny of Pakistan.

September 2

I have quite often thought that I am not suited for a Government job. There have been times I have felt unhappy. The circumstances of my early life forced me to accept a Government position as a drowning man will catch at a straw. It is not a question of money. I am not hungry for money. I have never dreamt of becoming a millionaire. I believe in having only that much that enables a man to lead a comfortable and easy life. By easy life I don't mean a life of ease. Government service is a dull and routine life. Merit hardly counts, particularly when you are working in a Mission abroad. You are at the mercy of the Head of the Mission and your immediate boss. There is no credit for what you do. All the credit goes to the man at top. A small increment once in a year is hailed as a momentous event in life, though by the time it comes the inflation has eroded the value of rupee. One clings to each paisa and breaks his head if unforeseen circumstances necessitate sudden expenditure not accounted for in the monthly pay.

But that is not all. The hard work of the year is summed up in the annual confidential report, which is seldom written on merit and is seldom based on honest and fair assessment. It all depends upon the likes and dislikes of the boss and more so of his better half, whose presence is as dominant as of her husband. Attending to the personal needs of the boss and his wife is more meritorious than writing good notes and expressing an honest opinion. If you voice your concern at the extravagant habits of your boss and his family, you are doomed for next promotion. I see much of waste, but I try to keep my eyes closed and ears plugged. I am not a social reformer. I wish I could be one.

The intelligence and consequently the utility of a man in Government service is measured by his rank. The lower the rank, the most stupid and unintelligent the man is rated. This is the system that we have perhaps inherited from the British when they ruled us. Or may be it is ingrained in human nature. Nobody tries to understand the background and the circumstances of the life of his subordinate particularly one at the lower end of the ladder. Should we expect anyone to have such an understanding?

September 4

Every time we go to the market to buy groceries and other essential items of daily use, there is an increase in price of every commodity. During the last three months the price of rice has gone up by 22%, soap 33%, eggs 25%, dals 20%, spices 30 to 40%, sugar 8% (despite a glut in the market) and meat 10%. It is difficult to calculate increase in the prices of vegetables and fruits because these are seasonal items. Prices of imported goods during the same period of three months have gone up by 50% on an average and of medicines by 25 to 50%. Most of the canned stuff like jams and jellies, soups, tea, beverages, ovaltine, coffee, cocoa, juices, talcum powder etc is imported. Due to restrictions on the availability of free foreign exchange, the prices of these commodities have shot up.

September 5

Unemployment is on the increase because of fall in production and the consequent retrenchment of workers, without or with meager compensation, is posing a law and order problem. More than 10,000 men from the labour force have been dismissed or retrenched in Sindh province alone. The number of labourers retrenched or laid off in other provinces is not known. Many textile mills have been closed down. The retrenchment has affected various kinds of industries, such as, textiles, sewing machines, readymade garments, silk fabric, furnishings, chemicals, toilet goods, steel, medicines, vehicles, bicycles, rubber, cooking oil, paints, and many other which produce items of daily consumption.

In her sustained effort to earn foreign exchange, the Government of Pakistan has exported accumulated stocks of cotton leading to a rise in the domestic price.

Despite efforts by the Government the three factions of the Muslim League have not merged. This has given hope to Bhutto's Pakistan Peoples' Party to form the Government. But because of large scale retrenchment of workers in mills and industries, the image of Bhutto, who is considered to be the champion of labour class, is bound to suffer in the public eye. In one way he is perhaps right that he has no power or authority to deal with the situation, but he has to make a vocal protest, which he may not like at this juncture for fear of being put behind the bars. Perhaps he is on the horns of a dilemma. If he does not raise his voice, he is going to lose the sympathy and goodwill of the electorate. And if he does, in the name of maintaining law and order in the country at this hour of national crisis of frightening magnitude, the martial law authorities will have the least hesitation in curbing his activities and stifling his voice. To do or die – the question looms large before him. He does not seem to have a ready answer. He is groping in the dark for a ray of hope and a current of fresh air to repair his damaged lungs.

September 10

The proposed visit of Yahya Khan to Tehran has an element of mystery. No date has been announced, nor the duration of his visit known. Is he going for military hardware or for economic aid or for much-needed cash? It is anybody's guess.

Bhutto has become vociferous. He has threatened the military regime with dire consequences if power is not transferred to him immediately. He says openly that he will not allow factories, schools and banks to function nor permit the farmers to pay rent to the rich landlords and the taxes to the Government. The last and final round of talks, as it is made out, between him and Yahya Khan is still to be held. But the indications are Bhutto is inviting trouble for himself.

The Textile industry is the hardest hit. Many looms have been declared non-functional deliberately to avoid taxes, which are levied on capacity or actual production whichever is higher.

The conditions in East Pakistan are still chaotic. The trade between the two wings virtually remains suspended. Even Dacca is not safe. Murders take place in broad daylight. Jamat-e-Islami and Pakistan Peoples' Party have already blamed each other for killing workers belonging to their respective parties in East Pakistan.

For more than three months the foreign office in Islamabad has not issued any exemption certificate allowing us to import articles of daily use from abroad. The last certificate was issued on May 29. This is causing great hardship to our people in the High Commission. Life in Karachi has become dull and boring.

Can Pakistan have democracy? This question is in the minds of many people. If so, when? That is another question. When Ayub Khan took charge of the Government, he had perhaps correctly said, "...democracy unfortunately is unavailable to most of the Muslim countries". For a long time political bankruptcy has created a vacuum, which cannot be filled in so easily particularly when there is hardly any leader of caliber. The one who had caliber is already in jail and the one who has some may be in jail any time.

Ever since the creation of Pakistan a systematic campaign of hatred has been launched against India by all and sundry in West Pakistan. This campaign is carried out to the extent of open abuse and spite. Even Ayub Khan had said about Nehru that he was a liar and a dishonest man. Bhutto abused India openly in the Security Council. Yahya Khan has used highly offensive language against Prime Minister Indira Gandhi. The entire publicity effort is directed towards one end – HATE INDIA.

On my return flight from Delhi on September 7, while I was on courier duty, I happened to meet Mr. Javeed, First Secretary in the Pakistan High Commission in New Delhi. He talked nicely, though briefly. One impression that I gathered from him was that he felt at ease in Delhi contrary to what we felt in Karachi. There is much difference between the treatment meted by India to the Pakistan High Commission diplomats and officials in New Delhi and the treatment meted out to our Missions in Islamabad and Karachi.

The local CID (Pakistan Intelligence Bureau) questions everybody who visits our High Commission. Their methods are rough and crude. If anyone visits us two or three times, he is a worried man. There were times when our library was crowded with Pakistani visitors, many of them were students, who came to read Indian newspapers and magazines and borrowed books. Nobody visits now. Our library wears a deserted look.

September 11

While we in India think of our future and shed no tears on the past, in Pakistan the people woefully muse on the past. On the death anniversary of Qauid-e-Azam Mohammed Ali Jinah, the founder of Pakistan, one can notice a feeling of frustration in the writings of people connected with the movement for the creation of Pakistan and in newspaper editorials. It is felt Pakistan is miles away from the goal laid down by the late Quaid-e-Azam. Democracy has been stifled. People have no voice. The rich are becoming richer and the poor are becoming poorer. Unemployment has increased. Facilities for rural education and rural uplift are still lacking. People see "death in life". There is no national spirit and sense of dedication. Everyone is interested in his self and personal glory. Looting, murders and violence – stories of the past are still valid today. There are mutual rivalries and divergent ideologies within Islam.

This kind of frustration in Pakistan is bound to increase day by day. Religion may be a consolation, but hardly a binding force as is amply proved by the risings in East Pakistan. Religion in this country, as a matter of fact, has been used as a bait to catch the poor. Pakistan was painted as a paradise for Muslims on earth before her creation, and today when people have got fed up with the existing order, the responsibility for chaotic conditions is put on God as if He willed it that way. Is He the same God who created Pakistan or is He a different God? Only God knows.

Mr. Kotwal, the Legal Adviser to late Quaid-e-Azam in a televised speech said that what Jinah wanted was practising religion and not merely teaching. Unfortunately the contrary has been happening. He blamed the men in high positions who lived in a secluded world of their own, inaccessible to the common man.

September 12

Islam has ceased to be a binding force in Pakistan. The events in East Pakistan have proved this and now Khan Abdul Wali Khan has said that Islam cannot keep the two wings united. Islam was a strategy for creating Pakistan and for bringing the Muslims together under the same banner. But the myth has been exploded.

One High School teacher when questioned on the ideology of Pakistan gave a candid reply that it was meant to divide Pakistan into two parts. Prof. Ghulam Azam of Jamat-e-Islami, East Pakistan, has expressed serious doubts if democracy can survive in Pakistan.

Prices of essential commodities have further gone up. Compared with prices four months ago, fish has gone up by 100%, onions 100%, chicken 50%, eggs 40% and soap 33% - to mention a few.

September 13

Some people think power may eventually be transferred to Bhutto as he has the support of working classes, the farmers and even the students. It is said that he has also the support of some rich people and the Punjabis. They are perhaps the people who have no clout with the Military regime. He met Yahya Khan today. The outcome of their talks is not known.

Some people think if there is trouble in West Pakistan similar to one at present in East Pakistan, the situation will be so chaotic and uncontrollable as to lead to anarchy.

September 14

It is now reported that the three-hour talk yesterday between Bhutto and Yahya Khan that concluded at two in the afternoon was inconclusive. Poor Bhutto was not even served lunch. It is strongly rumoured that, as warned by Yahya Khan, if Bhutto does not remain within his limits, he may find himself behind bars. What does this mean? It means, as assessed by some, that Bhutto should keep his loud mouth shut and stop demanding restoration of democracy and as a consequence the transfer of power to him.

A break in diplomatic relations between Pakistan and India is not ruled out. Of course, the first move will be from Pakistan side. Pakistan has an apprehension that India has given a *de facto* recognition to Bangladesh by allowing her to open an office in Delhi, giving permission to her leaders to hold meetings and conferences in India and helping her in many other ways.

Much is being said in the media about Rashid Minhas, who has been posthumously conferred with the title of Nishan-e-Hyder, the highest civilian award in Pakistan. From his photographs appearing in the newspapers and the descriptions given, it seems his father Abdul Majid Mian is a highly influential man and in Pakistan influence counts much. Rashid did not belong to a poor family as is made out. His father, a rich man, lives in a beautiful villa. Some people say that Rashid Khan was an eccentric fellow, who invited death for himself. Strangely, the citation does not clearly spell out the merits of Rashid that entitled him to the award.

Lest Bhutto should spread unrest and create trouble, patrolling by the police in Karachi has been intensified. But this is not the first time Bhutto has threatened to intensify his campaign against Yahya Khan and the Military Regime. Nothing is likely to happen.

September 17

An article by Mir Laik Ali on "India's Occupation of Hyderabad" is somewhat mellowed in tone. It reflects, to a large extent, the frustration of all those who migrated from India to Pakistan. They still have no recognition, no merit and no voice. Over and above they all feel that whereas the Muslims of Hyderabad were in the forefront of demand for Pakistan, they have been woefully neglected after the creation of Pakistan. Laik Ali has no hesitation in saying that it was "The State of Hyderabad that had rendered vital services to so many Muslim countries all over the world (especially Pakistan) – a state to which Pakistan must remain indebted for support at many of its crucial moments at the cost of Hyderabad". These gestures of goodwill and support included a sum of rupees twenty crore that the Nizam of Hyderabad donated to Pakistan.

In another article Ibrahim Jalees says that when he sees an old man wearing a Turkish cap and a buttoned up wide-collared sherwani, he feels the spirit of Hyderabad is wandering restlessly on the roads of Pakistan. His complaint is that Hyderabad has not been equated with Junagarh in extending recognition and courtesy to the people who migrated from Hyderabad.

The lies told by Pakistan have no bounds. The latest diatribe is that detunes in Kashmir, kept in concentration camps, are given electric shocks and are subjected to many torturing methods including rubbing of salt on their wounds by the Indian army in order to extract confessions from them.

Many people have praised the decision of the Government in delinking rupee from sterling pound. They consider it a bold step. But Dr. Anwar Iqbal, the former Economic Adviser to the Government of Pakistan, has criticized the decision branding it hasty and unwarranted. He feels that the decision was taken because of the unfriendly attitude of the British Government.

The refrigerator that I had ordered from abroad had been lying with the Karachi customs for three months for want of exemption certificate from the Pakistan Foreign Office. It was eventually cleared today.

September 18

Bhutto could not be traced anywhere yesterday. He left home at 7 a.m. and was supposed to return by 7 p.m. Till as late as 11 p.m. his domestic servant had no news of him. He was reported to have met an important visitor at his Malir bungalow. In normal circumstances this would not have been news. The present conditions of uncertainty lead to all sorts of rumours and speculations. The details of the important visitor, Bhutto is alleged to have met, are not known.

The West Pakistanis have certainly no soft corner for the Bengalis. Everyone has ridiculed Sheikh Mujib to the extent of open abuse and meanness.

The military tribunal trying Sheik Mujib is reported to have completed its proceedings and is likely to submit its report to Yahya Khan in near future. Everything is shrouded in mystery.

Some realization has dawned on some of the intelligent people in Pakistan that in the name of Islam much harm has been done to the society. In the name of Islam bribery, black-marketing, corruption and favoritism are being practised in broad daylight without any fear of the Government and even that of God. Islam is no longer a guiding and binding force as it was before the creation of Pakistan.

September 19

The conditions in East Pakistan are still chaotic. The appointment of Dr. Malik has failed to restore confidence among the Bengalis. Shops are closed at dusk and people like to go home in daylight. The factories and the mills are still not working satisfactorily. The workers are afraid of coming to work. No trains are running from Dacca to outlying districts. The rail link between Dacca and Chittagong is still cut off. There are so many breaches that the repairs at this point of time are out of question. The jute mills are not working even to half the capacity partly because of shortage of raw jute and partly because of lack of full-fledged cooperation from the labour force. The Military authorities requisition public services without any compensation. There is a widespread feeling that Pakistan will not be able to retain its Eastern link.

The Bengalis living in West Pakistan are in a miserable plight. They are treated as third rate citizens and are openly abused. All Bengalis have been removed from the key posts both in the Government and in public offices. Most of them want to get out of West Pakistan, but they cannot. All roads are blocked. The lucky ones have already escaped to East Bengal in the hope of breathing free air as and when Bangladesh becomes a reality.

September 23

Bhutto has proved to be a coward. He had sometime back openly declared that by the end of September either the power will be transferred to him or he will go to jail. He knew he could not get power and at the same time he did not want to go to jail.

Now, he has pushed the date to the 1st of January, without of course mentioning the year.

September 24

The danger of famine in East Pakistan has been averted due to timely aid by the U.S.A. Dacca has a ring of protective military force. That is why Dacca is comparatively safer than most of the other parts of East Pakistan. There is a growing discontentment among the people.

It is stated that Pakistan has compensated Iran for the demonetized currency, but not Afghanistan because the latter is not militarily strong and Pakistan cannot expect any help from her.

Pakistan is exporting high quality rice to earn foreign exchange. The domestic price of good rice (not top quality, which is exported) has considerably gone up. Open adulteration of atta, ghee, rice and other items of food has become very common. Earlier the shopkeepers were mortally afraid of the military regime for indulging in unfair trade practices, such as, adulteration, short measure and selling in black market; now they are not.

There is a considerable fall in jute production in East Pakistan. This is partly attributed to non-availability of seeds and loans from the banks and partly due to the fact that many jute growers have switched over to growing of rice which fetches better price.

Broken rice of inferior quality is being sold at rupees 40 to 45 per maund (roughly 35 kg), whereas good quality rice is available at double the price. Sugar is being sold at rupees 2.75 per seer. Similarly, prices of all essential commodities have skyrocketed in East Pakistan. In short, in roughly three months time the prices of most of the essential commodities have almost doubled.

September 25

In spite of the fact that very few Hindus are left in West Pakistan, the anti-Hindu propaganda never ceases. A few days ago a news item appeared that some Hindus move about in suspicious circumstances in certain areas of Sind. Today, it is mentioned in the Hurriyet that two Hindu widows sold their property in violation of "Principle of Hindu Law" and after illegally transferring the money they went over to India. The sale deeds show only Rs 30,000 where the reporter says the property is worth lakhs. It is a fantastic allegation. The total area sold is roughly 800 sq.yd. The highest price of land in Karachi is Rs 40 per sq.yd. The building itself is old. How the sale can run into lakhs of rupees, only the prejudiced mind of the reporter knows.

The newspapers are gradually reporting acts of violence and sabotage in East Pakistan. One foreign vessel loaded with wheat was badly damaged in the port of Chalna. The son of Fazal-ul-Qadar Chaudhry, a prominent Bangali leader, was fired at by some miscreants, receiving injuries in the leg and the abdomen.

After living in Karachi for a few months and reading the newspapers both in English and Urdu I have a strong feeling that vulgarized and abusive anti-India propaganda systematically carried out by the media in collaboration with the Government and the politicians will leave such bitter memories of my stay in Pakistan that I will not be able to forget for many years to come. The Pakistanis consider themselves to be true Muslims, but in the name of religion they commit all sorts of sins and crimes. They have no moral scruples.

September 26

Bhutto is gradually realizing that democracy in Pakistan has to be written off. He has said that if the National Assembly does not meet in December 71 or January 72, the people of Pakistan should say "goodbye to democracy". His wish of "goodbye" is more likely to be granted by Allah through courtesy of Yahya Khan.

September 28

The weekly Nustrat of the 26th on its front page carried the photo of a Hindu recluse with a string of thick coloured beads round his neck, top-knot hanging loosely on the shoulder, body smeared with ashes, a red-coloured thick bangle on his arm, supporting only a loin cloth and smoking chilam (a contrivance made of clay for smoking tobacco). The caption is "Bramhni Smaj (Hindu priestly class) became naked".

Incidentally on the same day in the evening when I went out for a stroll, I saw a semi-starved, stark-naked Muslim sitting on the roadside. I wish I could show this to the man who painted the picture of an Indian sadhu to ridicule Hindu community in India. It is a pity that in Pakistan most of the writers, artists, politicians and religious leaders ridicule Hindu society without first searching their own hearts and without analyzing the deep-rooted evils in their own society.

Laik Ali, the former Prime Minister of Hyderabad during the last days of Nizam, who was instrumental in donating twenty crore rupees to Pakistan just after the partition of India, migrated to Pakistan on the fall of Hyderabad to India. He had come with high hopes of getting some high position in Pakistan but is spending the last days of his life cultivating land in the hottest part of Sind.

Haji Ibrahaim Sattar, once called the Seth Sahib of Delhi, who left India on Jinah's invitation and transferred his liquid assets to Pakistan, is seen in Bori Bazar or Empress Market in torn shoes and with an old bag in his hand for buying groceries. He is a dejected man.

Raja Mahmud Sahib, supposed to be a rich man in pre-partition days, came to Pakistan on August 14, 1947 of his own free will with patriotic feelings in the hope of getting a prominent place in the Muslim society, but soon got disillusioned and was forced to accept a mediocre job in the London Islamic Centre.

Habib Ibrahim Rahmit Ullah, once Pakistan's High Commissioner in London, a Minister and Governor, has renounced politics and is doing some petty business these days.

Pouring venom against India is not confined to writers and politicians only. In the foreword to Sharif Ali Mujahid's book

"Indian Secularism", Mr. I.H. Qureshi, Vice Chancellor of Karachi University has this to say: "The Muslims (in India) are looked upon with suspicion and hostility. They find it difficult to get into the Government service. Trade and industry do not employ them. Economically they have been ruined. The situation gets worse every day. Culturally it is expected of them to get assimilated into the general Hindu milieu. They are a community with no present, no future and no hope".

Democracy has little future in Pakistan. In India, as Raja Gazanfar Ali says, politically there was much difference between the Hindus and the Muslims. The Hindus already had political awakening, as they would vote for political or economic considerations. While the Muslims did not have much political awakening or more precisely were not conscious of the virtues of democracy before the creation of Pakistan. No efforts were made to educate them. It is now perhaps too late. Even if democracy is once again introduced, it will be short-lived. Nobody seems to listen to the warning of Nur-ul-Amin, a prominent Muslim leader, that if democracy is not restored in Pakistan, Pakistan may cease to exist as envisioned by her founders.

September 29

In his memoirs compiled by Sayeed Ahmed in the form of "Martial Law to Martial Law", Raja Gazanfar Ali speaks against India and her leaders (the sole exception is Gandhiji) with the same venom with which most of other Pakistani speak. But a few things he has revealed are quite interesting:

1. Jinah explained that he was a Shia (not Ismaili as generally understood), a believer in 12 Imams. His wife said she was also a Shia.

2. Gandhiji and Suhrawardy were instrumental in maintaining Hindu-Muslim amity and harmony.

3. Liaqat Ali Khan paid much attention to the defence of Pakistan. He spent lavishly on arms and ammunition for

the security of the country. When the Emperor of Iran visited Pakistan in 1950, he was much impressed by the parade of tanks, airplanes and naval ships.

4. In 1951, Abdul Rahman Azim Pasha, the Secretary General of Arab League sent a message to Liaqat Ali that in the event of an attack on Pakistan by India the entire Muslim world would be on the side of Pakistan.

5. Pakistan invited many businessmen from India to invest in that country.

6. Mr. B.K. Das, representative of the minority community in East Pakistan, it is alleged, used to consult the Deputy High Commissioner of India in Dacca. On the night of May 24, 1956, a meeting was called at the residence of the DHC where it was decided that negotiations with Abu-ul-Hassan Sarkar of the Muslim League should be broken and a compromise reached with the Awami League.

On Gandhiji, Raja Sahib says (translated from Urdu) that if we look at the complete political life of Ghandhiji, many facets of his character come to light. He was a Mahatma because of his chaste life, human brotherhood and high ideals. In the war for independence he armed the unarmed soldiers with moral strength. He was a General well versed in the game of political chess and an artist in the art of propaganda. He fought with every non-violent weapon to achieve his right goals. He never accepted the Two-Nation Theory. He considered people of all religious faiths as one family and one clan. But he laboured under a wrong impression that the twenty crore people of India had the same mental and emotional make up as he himself had. Like a professional chess player he countered any move by the Muslims based on the Two-Nation theory. Judging from the results achieved there were no political differences between his outlook and the outlook of a fanatic Hindu. In the last five-six months of his life he proved that the objective of his political life was religious fanaticism."

On the contrary like many other Muslims in Pakistan, Sadiq Ali Khan in his book Betegh Sipahi (Swordless Soldier) talks of Gandhiji in derogatory words, "Mahatma Gandhi made the most of every opportunity that projected him through media in other countries. Just to show to the world he observed a fictitious fast unto death. But that was good for Pakistan. She got fiftyseven crore rupees from India".

Sadiq Ali makes some interesting observations in his book:

1. The present generation in Pakistan is not so familiar with the horrible past, and the difficulties, misfortunes and atrocities faced by their ancestors and the desirability of establishing Pakistan as they should be. Often many Pakistani young men have been heard saying that India was divided without any justification which resulted in enmity between the Hindus and the Muslims. Some Muslims who did not have any connection with the past sometimes ask if creation of Pakistan was a right thing.

2. Bande Matram (the national song of India) is in fact a prayer and a slogan. The Hindus of Bengal started a political movement to establish a Hindu Raj and to annihilate Muslim rule. They took an oath that unless they succeeded in their aim they would not rest. This song was sung to arouse the Hindus to bring them to a common platform so that they might burn the Muslim habitations, pillage and kill the Muslims. This song has a lot of idol-worship and incites to murder.

3. The Nizam of Hyderabad felt much insulted when Jinah started smoking in his presence. In order to teach him a lesson Nizam told Jinah that the question of Sir Mirza Ismail was his internal matter. The meeting broke off.

4. Many Memens and Kutch Muslims left all their possessions in India and migrated to Pakistan because of threats posed by Sardar Patel. On the other hand, the Hindus were allowed to take everything including even a parrot's cage and grinding stone when they migrated to India. (What a freak of imagination!)

5. Our unfortunate brethren (the Muslims) in India are in such a miserable condition that when one hears their stories, one is stunned. Whenever the majority community wants, these Muslims are sacrificed to Goddess Kali and whenever necessary, they are thrown across the border like sheep and goats.

6. Qaid-e-Azam Jinah married a Parsi woman after she embraced Islam. They had a daughter. Jinah wanted her to marry a Muslim but she refused.

7. Jinah had a sickly constitution. He had all the ills of heart, lungs and stomach. He did not pay attention to his health. He had attacks of pneumonia and was a patient of tuberculosis before he died.

8. The history of Pakistan tells that minorities should be treated with due respect. That is why there were no Hindu-Muslim riots in Pakistan (a pathetic fallacy). On the contrary every day in India the blood of Muslims is considered cheaper than water. In Pakistan members of minority community have always held high positions and are still holding high positions. We are proud of the minority communities.

   There was hardly any minority community worth mentioning left in Pakistan after the communal riots in the wake of the partition. The Hindus were either killed or forced to migrate to India.

9. The murderer of Liaqat Ali Khan was an Afghan. The USA refused to lend the services of her intelligence agency

on the plea that it was possible the relations between the two countries might deteriorate after the report was published.

The implication of this is not clear.

10. Sheikh Abdullah went to Delhi to talk to Nehru in order to settle Kashmir issue. But simultaneously he sent two of his confidents, namely, Bakshi Ghulam Mohammed and G.M. Sadiq to Pakistan. Later on they were called back to Delhi (presumably on the assurances of Nehru)
11. After accession of Kashmir to India, Sardar Patel (the Home Minister) made an offer to Quaid-e-Azam that if he agreed to reverse his views on the alliance to Junagarh, Manawar and Mangrol and did not side with Hyderabad, the Kashmir issue could be carried further.

In another book "*Indian Secularism*" by Sharif Ali Mujahid, only one-sided views are expressed. He does not have the moral courage to state the contrary viewpoint. Everybody knows that pre-partition riots took place throughout undivided India, but the author gives details of riots that took place in India after August 15, 1947. He gives instances of discrimination against the Muslims in service compared to the Hindus, the Christians and other minority communities. Either he does not know or hides his ignorance that the number of educated Hindus, Christians and other minority communities in Pakistan in proportion to the total population is much less than the number of educated Muslims in India to the total population of the Muslims. He quotes only those articles and dispatches that suit his purpose of vilifying India. But Joseph Lelyveld, the *New York Times* correspondent in his dispatch published in the New York daily on October 28, 1968 has correctly said that "Every time Muslims in India suffer some misfortune, it is magnified in Pakistan and taken as a proof of what is held to be the menace of the Hindu chauvinism. Thus, though the Indian Muslim is much less conspicuous than he was 21 years ago, he remains a basic element in the subcontinent's conflicts."

A Pakistani intellectual feels uncomfortable when an Indian Muslim greets another with folded hands or studies Hindi or acquires the habits of a Hindu, but he expects a Pakistani Hindu to do exactly what a Muslim does. Many of these so-called intellectuals in Pakistan have pervert minds. Instead of trying to create harmony between India and Pakistan, they are fanning the fire of communalism in India. If they leave the Muslims of India alone to manage their own affairs, most of the problems will be automatically solved. But that they will not, because the existence of Pakistan depends upon unabated hatred against India.

September 30

Bhutto's address to a largely attended Press conference revealed some interesting facts:

1. "In the national interest I pressed President Yahya Khan on the 11th of February in Rawalpindi to permit us about six weeks time to make an earnest endeavour to arrive at a settlement with the Awami League, but instead the Assembly was summoned on the third of March".
2. "East Pakistan is in flames, the whole country is in near ruin. How will Pakistan be rescued if new fires are to erupt in other parts of the country?"
3. Mr. Bhutto reiterated if the democracy was not restored before the end of the year, it would be too late to salvage and save Pakistan.
4. Mr. Bhutto quoted as President Yahya saying that as the country was nearly at war with India, he (Yahya Khan) could not go further to meet Pakistan Peoples' Party demands.
5. "I am not giving ultimatum or threats. I am too small a person to extend threats. I am only putting forth the reality and melody of politics".
6. Referring to the general amnesty, Bhutto said that it had been granted in the midst of a crisis. He added that if

"fascists, secessionists" and those who had been described as enemies of Pakistan were to be pardoned, there seemed no reason why "peasants and labourers here are detained" for seeking their rights or why students, poets and professors should be arbitrarily arrested and lashed.

7. Referring to what Mr. Bhutto described as "mistakes and miscalculations over the past twentythree years" he said "President Yahya Khan's regime had tried to tackle the accumulated mistakes, but he has been caught in the vortex".

One Mr. Iqbal Sujan, Assistant Commissioner of Noakhli even though in possession of a valid travel document was arrested at Karachi airport on the suspicion of escaping from the country. There is no specific charge framed against him.

Bhutto says that his party favours an open trial of Sheikh Mujib because his party did not know how much Awami League was in collusion with India or any other country

October 1

The discontentment among the public because of steep rise in the prices of essential commodities and seeming perpetuation of military rule is gradually mounting. Some people do not mind accusing Pakistan and even Yahya Khan. Growing unemployment, retrenchment of factory workers and slump in the market are also factors responsible for general discontent. The Government is trying her best to keep the prices of essential commodities in check, but that is not the only problem.

The Government of Pakistan has once again put restrictions on the exit of the officials of our Missions in Islamabad and Karachi. This is in retaliation to the alleged kidnapping of four personnel of the Pakistan High Commission in New Delhi (another fabricated story). It is almost five months when these restrictions were first imposed and none of us was certain when the restrictions would be lifted. We heaved a sigh of relief when an agreement was reached with India a few days ago to lift the restrictions. Now, once again the situation has become tense. Some officials who were to proceed on leave on the third and sixth of the month have to stay back.

October 2

Short of solitary confinement, life in general for us is insipid. We have no entertainment. We have no local friends. We have no place to go. Our movements are restricted – limited from home to office and back except picking up articles of daily use from the market on way back. At the most we can visit our own people from the Commission. This is in sharp contrast to life in Tokyo, where I served in the Embassy from May 1964 to July 1969 as Commercial Attachı. We were free to go anywhere we wanted. No permission was required. We could see many places of historical interest. There was lot of fun and activity. There was a lot of hustle and bustle everywhere. The Japanese were proverbially polite and friendly. Though a substantial majority of the Japanese did not know or knew very little about India, yet those who knew had a great regard for Indians. The anti-India stance, noticeable in Pakistan, did not exist there. We breathed free air and traveled even late at night without any fear and feeling of alienation.

October 3

Sometimes a reporter in Pakistan picks up a story from a dreamland. Referring to the theft of documents and personal belongings of the UN Relief and Rehabilitation Officer J.R. Kelly from the hotel room in Lahore, a reporter Sajjaid Kirmani alludes to the presence of an official of the Indian High Commission in Pakistan "staying in the same hotel on that particular night". The fact is that no official of the Indian High Commission is permitted by the Pakistan Government to break journey at an intermediate point and as a matter of fact nobody from the High Commission stayed there.

Pakistan has come out with another fantastic story. A million-dollar exchange racket is linked with the hijacking of the India Fokker Friendship plane on January 27. The racket, as alleged, involves ten Pakistani business firms, two each in Karachi, Lahore and Peshawar, three in Rawalpindi and one in Dacca.

There is one industry that is thriving in Pakistan – the industry of manufacturing lies both for export and domestic consumption. But in spite of free distribution as a charity, there are a few right-thinking people who have no taste for it. Still, as it appears, most of the Pakistanis take the lies on their face value and perhaps enjoy it as they enjoy dates and mangoes freshly plucked from the trees.

October 5

Ibrahim Jalees, a columnist of the daily *Hurriat* is on a visit to East Pakistan. He has revealed or confirmed that:

1. Armed guards in plain clothes accompany each flight from Karachi to Dacca and back.
2. Military personnel move in civilian clothes from Karachi to Dacca as on their arrival at Dacca airport an announcement is made: "Persons connected with the military should report themselves at the airport counter".
3. At the Intercontinental Hotel, the baggage of each person is searched to detect any concealed arm or ammunition before he is allowed to move to his room.
4. On every Government and non-Government building, the green flag flutters.

Pakistan is trying to export everything possible – vegetables, meat, poultry, basmati rice, sugar, cement, raw cotton, textiles and any agricultural produce acceptable anywhere in the international market at the cost of starving her own people. She needs foreign exchange badly to build up her military strength.

October 7

It is strange that those who migrated from India are still considered refugees, even though some of them are quite prosperous and doing good business. There is a lot of discrimination between one class of persons belonging to one province or community or even a sect and the other. A Punjabi will prefer to employ a Punjabi, a Sindhi a Sindhi, a Sunni a Sunni, a Shia a Shia, and so on.

The Ministry of Information has distributed pamphlets and posters marked as CRUSH INDIA and CONQUER INDIA to be displayed on all sorts of public and private vehicles to whip up war-hysteria. Troops with arms and ammunitions have already been moved to the borders with India and one can notice air activity too.

October 8

Does a common man in Pakistan really want democracy? It is hard to answer one way or the other. Till 1958 when Martial Law was imposed for the first time, it is said, that the common man had seen so much of misery and hardship inflicted on him by the politicians that he now shudders at the very thought of democracy. But on the contrary he has seen too much of highhandedness during the military regime that he cannot make up his mind what is preferable – democracy or military rule? He cannot appeal to any authority for injustice done to him by a bureaucrat or even by an ordinary policeman. Otherwise the magnitude of corruption, exploitation, injustice and cruelty remains the same whether it is democracy or military rule in Pakistan.

Most of the West Pakistanis are gradually coming to believe that East Pakistan has become a liability and Pakistan would do better if she were left with West Pakistan only. So much blood is being shed in the name of religion. So much energy is being wasted. And so much of public money is being squandered on East Pakistan just for the sake of unity which was not there and which will not be there.

October 10

It is now confirmed by Raza Kasuri, the Chairman of Pakistan Peoples' Party (Raza Group) that certain elements in West Pakistan "are lobbying with the military regime that if East Pakistan has to go, it might as well go today". The reasons are obvious. Pakistan is spending much in East Pakistan with no return and with no assurance of any return and normalcy in future.

The lifting of ban on political activity is another eyewash. There are so many ifs and buts attached to Martial Law Regulation 94 that any political activity carried in any manner will come under threat of action by the military regime.

October 11

Many businessmen in West Pakistan have lost business in East Pakistan because the only place where they can sell their merchandise is Dacca. There is too much risk of life in carrying on business in other parts of East Pakistan because of volatile conditions. Almost 60% of the goods manufactured in West Pakistan were sold in East Pakistan from where some of them found their way to India because West Pakistan cannot sell direct to India.

Master Khan Gul, the Vice-President of the defunct Awami League has come out with a statement that India did not interfere in the internal affairs of East Pakistan prior to March 25, 1971. He is of the view that Mujib is not responsible for the East Pakistan debacle. He has blamed Bhutto for creating a gulf between the two wings.

Anti-India propaganda coupled with cries of war is gaining momentum day by day and hour by hour. It appears most of the people in West Pakistan have gone mad or have lost their mental poise. India is being depicted a land of callous Hindus, whose women do not love their husbands but are fond of Muslims. India has no scruples about Geneva Convention when treating prisoners of war. The Muslims in India have become slaves to the Hindus and have no love for Islam. The Indians are misers and have no sense of justice and fairness.

It is a pity that every evil in Pakistan society is attributed to India. One Aqil Ahmed Khan Lodhi writing on the evil of dowry traces its origin to the Hindu religion. He says in the Hindu society the birth of a daughter is looked down upon. After her marriage she is considered as good as dead. But then he admits that dowry is a greater evil in Pakistan. Hundreds of parents have become mad and committed suicide because they could not give dowry to their daughters.

October 12

Retired Air Marshal Asghar Khan, the Chief of Tehrik-e-Istaqlal has come out with plain speaking and forthright statements. His press statement on October 6 in Dacca was totally blacked out under instructions from the Government. A few foreign correspondents (mostly from Muslim countries) present in the press conference had to go to Bangkok to send their dispatches.

Asghar Khan has criticized peace committees, whose members, he alleges, are thoroughly corrupt. He specifically refers to one member who could not afford to travel by rickshaw once, has now three cars. He talks of one Dr. Malik who criticized the appointment of ministers from among the defeated candidates in the elections.

He has warned the Government against its bureaucratic attitude and adds if need arises, he will not hesitate to break the law. He further says that there is something wrong somewhere in the East Wing Administration of Pakistan and if the wrong is not corrected immediately and effectively, it would be a misfortune for the country.

He has pleaded for freedom of press. He has said that one loyal to the country need not be loyal to the Government. In his forthright statement he said, "Unfortunately, in this country, anyone who refuses to toe the official line is branded as a traitor and the national press, instead of using discretion, portrays him in such a way as if he is really a traitor." He added that patriotism was not the monopoly of one man (an allusion is to Yahya Khan).

He has suggested setting up of a high-powered tribunal to probe into the factors which have brought a perfectly well-established country to the brink of ruination.

Today's Pakistan's President message to the Nation was a repetition of tirade against India. He seems to be afraid of war, but that may be a sign of nervousness regarding the consequences. One can never be sure of his intentions. Out of frustration due to political, economic and moral chaos in the country, he may eventually embark on this venture. In fact, some rumours are already afloat that war with India may break out sometimes in the latter half of October.

In his televised speech Yahya Khan drank water twice, visibly took a long breath a number of times and paused frequently to punctuate his sentences. He is comparatively short statured as compared to other Army Generals and is stocky built rather overweight. It is said that he drinks a lot of Scotch every night before he takes his dinner. His English is undoubtedly very poor. Despite the prepared speeches, in moments of excitement (that he often has when referring to India) he overlooks the written text and adds his own vocabulary outside a standard dictionary of English language.

October 14

Some criticism has been made of the indifferent attitude of relief and other charitable organizations in West Pakistan intended to mitigate the plight of the refugees in East Pakistan. Not a single person, not a single organization has expressed sympathy or rendered financial assistance to the refugees.

The water dispute between Sindh and the Punjab is assuming serious proportions. Some people have warned the Government that if immediate steps are not taken to settle the dispute, it may lead to a crisis equal in magnitude to the one in East Pakistan.

Bhutto cannot restrain himself from talking rubbish occasionally. His remark that the Islamic constitution has been framed by a non-Muslim has forced Justice A.R.Cornelius to resign from the post of Law Adviser to the President. Once again he has come out with the theory of rearranging borders with India so as to give Kashmir, Assam, Gurdaspur and Ferozepur in India's Punjab to Pakistan. He is surely living in a fool's paradise. Disgruntled as he is with the Military regime, some of his explosive and illogical expressions are perhaps excusable.

Bhutto has picked a quarrel with the Governor of Punjab over water dispute with Sindh and has warned him not to follow the divide and rule policy of the Britishers. An empty threat as usual.

Some teachers and students of the Karachi University arrested under Martial Law Regulations have been released as a result of amnesty granted by the Governor of Sindh. This includes a few Hindus.

A new type of poster has appeared: OPEN FIRE, FINISH INDIA, and CRUSH INDIA. Meetings are being organized to make people prepared for the emergency.

Occasionally a lone voice makes some kind of plain speaking. Kazi Mohammed Fazal of defunct Awami League has said that due to old bonds extending over thousand years, it is not possible to snap ties with India. Obviously, he has in his mind the Bengali culture, art and literature, food habits and language common between the two wings of Bengal. Almost all educated Muslims in East Bengal venerate Rabindranath Tagore as the Hindu Bengalis do.

October 16

How depraved the mind of a highly educated and a responsible person in Pakistan can be may be judged from the statement made by the retired Justice M.B. Ahmed and the former constitutional adviser to Jinah that India was involved in the conspiracy to murder Liaqat Ali Khan. He says (without bothering to verify the veracity of the statement) that one of his relatives, a woman, was told at the Delhi Airport not to go to Pakistan as Liaqat Ali was going to be murdered and India and Pakistan would become one.

Retired Major General Mohd. Akbar Khan Rangro has come out with a fantastic story. A few days before the murder of Liaqat Ali Khan, he alleges, an important meeting was held in a hotel (name not given by him) between Mr. Keskar, the Deputy Foreign Minister and some high officials of a neighbouring country including one well-known Kashmiri gentleman to hatch a conspiracy for the murder of Liaqat Ali Khan. When the conspiracy was being hatched, a Muslim bearer in the hotel overheard the conversation and immediately contacted the Pakistan High Commission in New Delhi, but nobody paid any heed to him.

None of these gentlemen who have come out with their own versions of the assassination of Liaqat Ali Khan have given any explanation why the police officer killed the assassin. In the same breath they also say that there were certain internal rivalries. It is said that Syed Akbar, the killer, was being closely watched by Pakistan Intelligence, but he still managed to shoot at Liaqat Ali Khan. It is obvious the conspiracy to eliminate him was hatched quite some time ago.

Begum Liaqat Ali Khan is still hoping that one day the honest people in Pakistan will unearth the conspiracy to kill her husband. She is still labouring under an erroneous impression that there are indeed some honest people in Pakistan.

Mian Mohamed Ali Kasuri, the Vice-Chairman of Pakistan Peoples' Party has suggested that the income earned from East Pakistan whether through internal resources or through exports should be spent on development in East Pakistan itself. It is strange he is putting forward the same proposal for which Mujib fought and was censured by the West Pakistan.

The coming elections in East Pakistan are going to be a farce as can be easily perceived from the statement made by Maulana Mufti Mahmud, General Secretary of Jamiat Ulma-e-Islam (Hazarvi Group) that the Ministers in Dr. Malik's cabinet have the support of the Government. It is also learnt that General A.A. Niazi is trying his best to Islamise the education system in East Pakistan, which means rubbing off of Bengali culture and language.

Mr. Sadiq Wahab of Pakistan Democratic Party has come out with a different theory that the conspiracy to murder Liaqat Ali Khan was hatched in Baluchistan. Mr. Wahab was arrested for expressing his views after Liaqat's murder.

October 17

Ian Stephens in his book "*The Pakistanis*" has more or less correctly judged the mind of Pakistan when he says, "Or you could turn the whole problem round, and say that what holds Pakistan together is something negative, not positive; not faith but fear. Fear of Hinduism, a political fear that without the British on the sub-continent as a third force, Islam there would be overwhelmed by it".

Most of the Pakistani Muslims are jealous (as they were before partition) of the intellectual superiority of the Hindus almost in every sphere and this jealousy has transformed itself into fear and fear into hatred. Every educated Muslim sincerely feels or gives an impression that India has never reconciled to the fact of creation and consequently the existence of Pakistan. It is doubtful if any right-thinking man in Pakistan has realised that by making India conscious of Pakistan's enmity towards her has inadvertently helped India in strengething her armed forces. Not only that, by dealing ruthlessly with her own peoples, that is, Pathans, Baluchis and now Bengalis, Pakistan has created dissension among her own ranks. Much noise was made in the name of Islam for creating Pakistan in accordance with the cardinal principles of Islam as laid down by Prophet Mohammed, but after Pakistan came into existence things have become worse. A natural question arises if, as vociferously alleged by the founders of Pakistan, in undivided India Hindus were the tormentors, why this injustice, exploitation, discrimination and pathetic disregard for the welfare of the common man, even twentyfour years after Pakistan came into existence, when there are no Hindus worth the name in Pakistan and when Pakistan is proclaimed an Islamic state based on Shariat laws?

October 23

Pakistan's victory over India in hockey is no doubt a matter of jubilation and an occasion for celebration on a big scale in Pakistan as by all and sundry, this is considered a victory over India in war. People do not bother if Pakistan lost the final match to Spain and drew with Holland. All that they wanted was that Pakistan should not lose to India and that has happened. One political leader has openly said that if Pakistan had lost, the defeat would have demoralised the people in general. One ex-soldier who fought in the 1965 war with India has said that in the battlefield India can never defeat Pakistan. In their exuberance of victory over India, the Pakistanis have forgotten their defeat by Spain.

There is no doubt that the activities of Bhutto's Peoples Party in East Pakistan are being blacked out both by the press and the radio, obviously at the behest of Yahya Khan.

Ex-Major General Akbar Khan, who was an accused in the Rawalpindi conspiracy case and is stated to be pro-Moscow, is active again in reorganizing the Peoples Guards, a para-military organisation and an offshoot of Peoples Party. On the ninth of the month he is reported to have held important discussions with extremist elements and leaders of Nationalist Students Federation, a leftist organisation. He is reported to have remarked that the

Peoples Guards will endeavour to liberate Kashmir by dint of sword and form second line of defence in case of war against India. He has suggested enrolment of extremist elements and formation of units in towns and cities where ex-servicemen reside in large numbers.

The special correspondent of the magazine *Zindgi* in October 18 issue says that Akbar Khan in collusion with Faiz Ahmad Faiz (a renowned Urdu poet), Sajjad Zahir and Mohd. Hussain Atta, tried to topple the Government of Liaqat Ali Khan and planned to set up a communist Government in Pakistan.

Nasim Akhtar, Chairman of the National Bank Employees Front, has said that only 5% of labour force has trade unions; the balance 95% is unorganized. The bureaucracy controlled by the capitalists has framed such laws as go against the interests of the labour class and suit only the industrialists and the capitalists. Eighty per cent of the population consisting of labourers, peasants and petty shopkeepers has no voice. There is not a single capitalist in Pakistan who does not own less than one dozen industrial units. If for any reason – shortage of raw materials, lack of demand or labour trouble, he has to close one unit that makes no difference to him. The law gives full freedom to the capitalist to dismiss any employee without assigning any reason. In the current crisis thousands of labourers in Karachi have been thrown out of employment and nobody has paid any heed to their difficulties and problems. Theirs is a cry in the wilderness.

October 24

Ibrahim Jalees, a columnist in daily *Hurriat* has treated the hockey match between India and Pakistan as the fourth battle of Panipat fought between the Babars of Pakistan and Rana Sangas of India. He adds that Pakistan's victory is a reflection of the past glory of the Muslims going back to 700 years when General Tark-bin-Ziad and Musa Bin Nasir hoisted the flag of Islam on the land of Spain. If this match had been played somewhere else, it could not have that importance. He thinks that it is a good omen for Pakistan because victory in the play field can prove victory in the battlefield. What a wishful thinking!

However, the editor of the paper admits that Pakistan's entry in semi-finals was also due to luck because Japan by defeating Holland by a solitary goal prevented Holland from entering into semi-finals. He says that in hockey Pakistan should not consider India as her only rival; other six nations have also come up.

October 29

The newspapers do occasionally give out stories of sabotage and bomb blasts in East Pakistan, though the coverage is limited to a few words without details.

It is not that easy to get authentic news in Pakistan. The newspapers do not correctly reflect the happenings in both the wings of Pakistan, particularly in East Pakistan. Everything is tailor-made. The press is not independent. All that appears in the media is inspired and dictated by the military regime.

The strength of our Missions in Pakistan is likely to be cut down because Pakistan has reduced the strength of her Missions in Delhi and Bombay. As a matter of fact, in the present circumstances of Pakistan's apparent hostility towards India, our Missions are not serving much useful functions because we have no contact with the local people. Our Library and reading room, which attracted a large number of Muslims, particularly the students starved of good books both in science and literature, are lying idle. Due to restrictions put on our movements outside Islamabad and Karachi, we have to sit idle at home. The visa work has been considerably reduced rendering the staff idle. The reduction is a logical step. But the question is when the surplus staff can leave.

October 31

It is over six months I have been here. Ever since my arrival each day has been one of anxiety and suspense. No one among us knows what is going to happen tomorrow. Nobody knows when we will get out of this state of anxiety, uncertainty and suspense. It is neither freedom nor imprisonment here. We are free because we belong to a Diplomatic Mission, but we are not free in the sense of moving about freely. It is a strange kind of mental unrest.

November 1

President Yahya Khan seems to be under pressure when he says, "If the nation demands his (Mujib-ul-Rahman's) release, I will consider doing it". He has also come out with maximum autonomy for the Bengalis except giving them defense, foreign affairs and taxation. It is, more or less, what the Awami League wanted. But no sensible man in East Pakistan will trust the military regime after so many innocent Bengalis have been bled to death. Judging from his past performance, any statement made by Yahya Khan, howsoever well-intentioned, lacks authenticity and appeal.

November 3

The televised interview of hockey players has revealed, among other things, that they have no spirit of sportsmanship though they claim to be world champions. For their defeat in early matches and in the final against Spain, they have blamed poor umpiring. The solitary goal scored by India was just a matter of chance whereas the goals scored by them was a team effort thereby suggesting that Indians were a disorganized lot.

November 5

China has reportedly supplied one hundred tanks and many heavy field guns to Pakistan. It is difficult to get any confirmation.

Some hundred eminent people of Pakistan are conducting a signature campaign for petitioning to Yahya Khan to release Mujib. It is reported that Retd. Air Marshal Asghar Khan is also trying to get Sheikh's release. It is doubtful if Yahya Khan, who once called Mujib a traitor, will let him breathe free air. The fate of

Sheikh is hanging in the balance. However, why Yahya Khan is delaying a decision on him is a matter of conjecture. Either he is hoping for reconciliation or he is under pressure from the world powers to free him.

In view of grave economic crisis some politicians, industrialists and capitalists are trying to transfer capital from Pakistan to other countries through unauthorized channels.

The wife of Sayed Hassan, a prominent Pakistan's Peoples Party leader, was spat at by a Maulana at Karachi Airport when she went to receive her husband returning from Dacca. Other workers were injured and manhandled by the followers of Jamat-e-Islami. The police, it is reported, was a mute spectator.

November 7

The merchant class in Pakistan call themselves true Muslims. They raise the prices of essential commodities by 50 to 75% during the holy Month of Ramzan and eat during daytime behind curtains drawn on the front doors of the restaurants. They weigh less. They measure less. A team of Labour Welfare Department raided certain cloth shops and booked many cloth merchants for keeping unapproved yardsticks. In the Empress Market the vegetable sellers have no scruples in weighing less, and of course big businessmen indulge in many malpractices including blackmarketing and adulteration.

Bhutto's acceptance of offer made by Yahya Khan to lead the delegation to China leaves no doubt in one's mind that Bhutto is power-hungry. It suits Yahya Khan too because at least for some time he can keep Bhutto's mouth shut and delay transfer of power to him. As a matter of fact Yahya Khan cannot afford to be visibly strict with political leaders like Bhutto and Retd. Air Marshal Asghar Khan in West Pakistan because his hands are full tackling the turbulent situation in East Pakistan.

Retired Air Marshal Asghar Khan and Retired Major General Nur Khan have been too critical of Yahya Khan and his military regime. Nur Khan, once an accused in the Rawalpindi Conspiracy Case, has stepped up his activities, though secretly.

Most of the foreigners living in Pakistan and members of Diplomatic Missions in Pakistan have already made plans to send their families back home in case of war between India and Pakistan. We, the members of India Missions in Pakistan, who will be directly involved and worst affected, have appealed to the Ministry of External Affairs to keep bare minimum number of people in Pakistan. Most of us have practically no work and fresh workload cannot be expected as long as situation remains abnormal and possibility of war persists. We have practically no contact with the outside world. Our office is like a remote inn on a deserted highway where occasionally a soul may come for a night stay. Most of us are living in a state of suspense. Many of us have packed up many times, unpacked, repacked and unpacked again. I have never seen so much dullness and anxiety in the office.

The anti-India poison has been injected systematically into the minds of fanatic Muslims in Pakistan in order to prepare them for war. The events of 1947 at the time of partition are being purposely and viciously projected through radio, television and the press in a manner as if a new Pakistan has to be created out of the ashes of the old. A pious dream indeed! The creation of a New Pakistan on the edifice of the old tottering structure is not going to change the general conditions in Pakistan because those who want to usher a new era of prosperity and freedom are worse than those who were in the forefront of creating Pakistan. Everybody seems to have his own axe to grind. Everybody seems to be perplexed and disillusioned. Emphasis is once again being laid on Allah, who created Pakistan as a special case and who will preserve it too. The name of Allah keeps the people mystified and satisfied giving free scope to the military regime to indulge in luxury through loot of the public exchequer.

For the last few days Pakistani newspapers have started giving out news of sabotage, bomb explosions and political murders in East Pakistan. This is either to give a semblance of freedom of press or to justify Pakistan's atrocities against her Bengali brethren or both. But this kind of information can have a negative effect too. It is bound to create scare among the West Pakistanis, who have interests in East Pakistan and others who are required to serve there though a majority of them for fear of reprisals from the Bengalis have already bid adieu to East Pakistan.

November 8

In all probability Bhutto and for that matter Pakistan has not achieved much from his visit to China as was expected. No doubt, criticism of India does find a prominent place in the statement made by Mr.Chi Pengfei, the acting Foreign Minister, but it does not assure Pakistan of much-sought help from China. Either China has not relied on Bhutto, who is just a private citizen and has no say in the Government or China does not want to get actively involved into any conflict when she has just been admitted to the UNO. China's effort, it is surmised, will be to assume the role of a peacemaker so as to minimize the influence of both the USA and the Soviet Union.

There is no doubt that the people in general in West Pakistan are psychologically afraid of an open conflict with India in spite of CRUSH INDIA campaign launched by the military regime actively backed by the media. The common man faced with ailing and failing economy causing tremendous slackness in business activity and generating more unemployment is worried about his daily bread. The country is not as united as she was in 1965. West Pakistan will have to fight by herself on both the fronts, which can pose formidable problems for the military regime.

The Punjabi element has dominated the scene too long. Their dominance at the centre is becoming unbearable for the people living in other provinces, that is, Sindh, Baluchistan and NWFP as it has already become unbearable for the Bengalis in East Pakistan. If this trend continues, the history of East Pakistan may be repeated in West Pakistan.

November 9

The chances of Pakistan taking the initiative in provoking war against India have not receded despite the USA's decision (which could be symbolic) to stop military aid to Pakistan and China's reticence to declare open support to Pakistan. Notwithstanding world criticism Yahya Khan has become so brazenly bold that he can swallow the bitterest of pills without giving an impression of discomfiture. He has got himself caught so much in the meshes of his own follies and blunders that by his own effort he cannot come out unscathed.

Although the bureaucrats, the industrialists and the army personnel do not like Bhutto, he has so far managed the show of his political acumen because he is apt in choosing words and phrases that besides creating a sense of humour appeal to the illiterate masses. Earlier his boastful utterances appealed to the Punjabis and the Sindhis, but of late it seems even the Baluchis and Pathans have come under his influence because they are fed up with the military regime. Yahya Khan has joined the ranks of Chengiz Khan and the Timurs who had no concern for human suffering and misery. As a show of their might and authority they ruled with an iron hand and that is what Yahya Khan is doing now.

U.K. Islamic Mission has put some interesting questions to the political leaders of Pakistan:

1. Will you or God rule over Pakistan?
2. Will you be servants of Pakistanis or their masters?
3. Will you try your best to introduce Islamic way of education in the Universities of Pakistan by banning Western type of education?
4. Will you try to uplift Islam through press and other means of communication?
5. Will you consider it your duty to ban import of pornographic literature and sexy films so that Millat-e-Islamia can

progress safely without losing its path? What will be your attitude to the non-Islamic and unconstructive films produced in Pakistan?

6. Will you raise you voice in favour of declaring Arabic as the national language so that entire Millat-e-Islamia becomes of the same language and of same ideas?

(Taken from weekly *Zindgi* Lahore of November 8)

One R.H. Raja, a Pakistani in Istanbul talks of a Turk who told him that West Pakistan had proved that East Pakistan and West Pakistan were different because of colour and race. He has lamented the lack of support to the Bengalis in hour of crisis by some Muslim countries.

Mr.G. Muin-ud-Din, Ex-Chief Election Commissioner has come out with a statement that much pressure was exerted on him by the Government of Pakistan to declare Ayub Khan successful during the presidential elections in 1965. Of course, he succumbed to the pressure and declared Ayub Khan the President of Pakistan.

Pakistan will always remain in the hands of a handful of people, who have risen or who aspire to rise to high positions, which they could not have even dreamt of in undivided India. Anti-India stance is so handy to them for exploiting the poor, the uneducated and the unfortunate masses that nobody in power or aspiring to be in power can give it up. India has to remain vigilant all the time as Pakistani leadership is planning to attack India by keeping alive and maintaining anti-India propaganda and hate-India campaign. Even if by any chance democracy is restored at this juncture, it is doubtful if there can be any meaningful dialogue, not to speak of lasting friendship, between India and Pakistan. The confrontation between India and Pakistan has acquired the same dimensions as between Palestine and Israel. India may be willing to extend a hand of friendship, but Pakistan will never because the very existence and survival of Pakistan depends on hatred for India that simultaneously fetches her dividends both from the USA and China in the form of Military and Economic aid.

It is a piquant and paradoxical situation that Jamat-e-Islami accuses Bhutto of being an Indian agent and Pakistan's Peoples Party accuses Jamat of being a part of Jamat-e-Islami of India that has supported the cause of Bangladesh. It is difficult to say who is anti-India and who is pro-India? But this verbal confrontation keeps the masses in good humour and adds spice to the dull political life in Pakistan.

In spite of daily propaganda against India carried by the media, quite often amounting to vulgarity and cheap sentimentality, we the members of diplomatic mission have not noticed any apparent hostility against us from the common man. Since quite a few people know us and recognize us as they come to us to get visa or we go to the market to buy groceries, they do not apparently show any anger and hatred. It is hard to say why? This attitude of indifference, because they do not talk to us about anything other than what is necessary to sell their merchandise, is rather puzzling.

People in general seem to be more concerned with their daily existence which is pathetic. The poor people who fought for the cause of Pakistan have realised that far from getting fair and just treatment as promised by Qaid-e-Azam, they are in a worse plight than perhaps they were in undivided India. Some of them might have an apprehensive feeling how it serves the cause of Pakistan by throwing mud at India. Is it not more desirable to set one's own house in order? History alone will answer these questions.

November 10

Bhutto's statement that in the present circumstances Pakistan should exercise restraint towards the big powers indicates where Pakistan stands today. It is doubtful if Pakistan has the concrete support of any country. Even China has advised for a political settlement with the Bengalis within the ambit of Pakistan. It is ironical that Yahya Khan has paid no heed to the advice rendered to him by many countries including the USA, the USSR, the UK and China to release Mujib-ur-Rahman and compromise with him. The situation in Pakistan is very precarious. Some dramatic development is likely in a few days' time.

Five technicians of Karachi Nuclear Power Station have disappeared mysteriously. One of them, Abid Hussain, has succeeded in escaping from Pakistan.

The feeling among West Pakistanis that East Pakistan should have some autonomy to choose her destiny is growing stronger. But the military regime has plugged its ears.

November 12

Bhutto is an expert in creating situations, which fetch him the most palatable food – popularity. It is amusing why his opponents should choose a dental clinic for a murderous attack on him. He has no protection from the police and if anyone wants to kill him, there is hardly any hurdle. He knows how to spin a yarn out of bare threads. It is, however, ironical why the same people who were shouting "Bhutto Zindabad" (long live Bhutto) suddenly switched over to "Bhutto Murdabad" (death to Bhutto), when he refused to come out of his room. Were they disgusted or was the entire drama orchestrated? It is said the same processionists burned the flag of Pakistan's People Party and dispersed of their own without the intervention of the police, who were the mute witness to the high drama.

Once a while a fellow turns up and stirs one's blood. A young Muslim, whose application for a visa was rejected, came to see me. He had migrated to Pakistan last year and as he mentioned in his visa application he wanted to go to India to see his ailing mother. He was angry why visa had been refused to him when, as he said, we were issuing visas to non-Muslims. I told him that we did not discriminate on grounds of religion. From the number of visitors to India, he should know that almost all of them were Muslims. We had been till recently issuing visas liberally, but because of mounting tension between the two countries, we had restricted the grant of visa to genuine people. This young man, although he looked mature, lost his temper and said I was being cruel to him. That stirred my blood (as a diplomat I accept my fault that I should not have lost my temper, but strangely that proved to be blessing in disguise) and I asked how the West Pakistanis felt when the military regime committed acts of barbarity on innocent and helpless Bengalis in East Pakistan. I pointed out to him while he felt so sore because he could not see his mother reportedly ill, but did he or for that matter any sensible Pakistani ever think of hundreds of young Bengalis eliminated in East Pakistan who would never see their fathers and mothers again? I suggested he should put this question to Yahya Khan why he had created a situation where West Pakistanis could not go to India as often as they wished. I reminded him how venomous and vicious propaganda carried by the media in Pakistan against India was also responsible for stopping the flow of traffic from Pakistan to India. The man suddenly became apologetic and was in tears. He said the refugees were the worst sufferers in Pakistan and it is they who had asked for a separate state for Muslims. After 24 years they were still called Mohajrs (refugees) carrying the burden of class hatred and prejudices.

The Pathans learnt the lesson of discrimination right after 1947 when Khan Abdul Qayyum Khan ordered soldiers to open fire on innocent Pathans to crush Badshah Khan's spirit. The Baluchis are bitter that their province has been totally neglected. The Sindhis are shedding tears over failing crops for lack of water diverted to the Punjab. The Bengalis are already in revolt. These are facts of history and a lesson, as someone said, that nations could not survive on negatives.

November 14

On my going through Bhutto's "*The Great Tragedy*" I have a feeling that Bhutto is a cunning man. But somehow Yahya Khan, because he is in power, has so far got the better of him and has kept him in check. Yahya Khan has his own game to play. He could have snubbed Mujib the moment he announced six-point programme, but that would have strengthened the hands of Bhutto. In other words, Bhutto would have found a partner in Mujib to work against Yahya Khan. Instead he detained Mujib on charges of conspiracy against Pakistan in collusion with India. Obviously, the General wanted to kill two birds with one stone. To a large extent he succeeded in his objective, though he might not have anticipated that the consequences could be disastrous.

Like any other political leader in Pakistan Bhutto cannot restrain himself from implicating India for East Pakistan debacle. He makes the usual allegation of India assisting and abetting the Bengalis in East Pakistan to revolt against Pakistan. He says, as most of the Pakistanis say, that India has never recognised the existence of Pakistan. He has however not quoted a single instance where India was a party to the dispute between the two wings of Pakistan before March 25.

Bhutto's remarks that Mujib had the support of Big Business and the capitalists and even bureaucrats in West Pakistan in order to liquidate leftist element in Pakistan, makes a curious reading. Only Bhutto is capable of such innovations. He attributes his own success in the elections to his popularity among the masses, whereas he alleges Mujib's success was due to circumstances and the backing of West Pakistan elite. He underrates the stature of Mujib, whereas he rates himself very high. Bhutto either is a past master in concocting tales or has bouts of political hysteria, or both.

In fact Bhutto tried to compromise with Mujib and to achieve that end he had a secret meeting with Mujib in Dacca that he did not disclose to Yahya Khan even when the latter asked him. But as it was not the intention of the military regime to transfer absolute power to "Bhutto and Mujib" combined, Bhutto retracted his earlier statements that he was in favour of a compromise with Mujib. Howsoever shrewd Bhutto may be, at this juncture he is a confused man. Since he keeps on shifting his stand, his utterances lack authenticity. Ho does not have a single track mind to stick to one ideology.

Many political leaders in West Pakistan had tried for a solution to the crisis in East Bengal. They knew that by prolonging negotiations with Mujib, the postponement of restoration of democratic rights, the delay in rectifying the mistakes made by Ayub Khan regime and further ignoring the legitimate demands of Bengalis for full autonomy would be perpetuating the confrontation. But unfortunately the military regime erred on the wrong side and ignored the advice of the well-wishers.

In the current situation of political turmoil in both the wings of Pakistan it must be clear to the Big Business and Industrialists in West Pakistan that even if full autonomy is granted to East Pakistan at this stage, it would be too late. Knowing fully the pathetic conditions in East Pakistan and the determined revolt by the Bengalis, they must have concluded they cannot go back to East Pakistan to reestablish their business. It will be a Herculean task to heal the wounds of the Bengalis, who have lost faith in the Muslims of West Pakistan.

November 15

The Ministry of External Affairs has eventually agreed to the repeated suggestions made by the Assistant High Commission in Karachi to drastically cut down the strength of our Mission so as to keep the minimum number of people. We have in fact a very large contingent because the security considerations oblige us to get the security guards, the chauffeurs and even the sweepers from India, whereas in other countries we employ local people to run daily errands and maintain our buildings. It would be very difficult to meet the daily needs of every person and look after their families in the event of a war between India and Pakistan that was very much in the air.

It was decided to send the first batch on the 18th, the earliest flight available from Karachi to Delhi. Indian Airlines, Air India and Pakistan International and some other airlines had already stopped their operations between India and Pakistan. Mostly we use Pan Am that has both Karachi and Delhi on its route.

I have been told to lead the second batch of staff members to Delhi by the next available flight that may be in another 2-3 days.

November 18

The first batch left by air in the early hours without any difficulty. So I feel assured that I would go too. It would be a pleasure to go back home. It would be a pleasure to get out of this place where right from the time of my arrival I felt uneasy particularly when I had left my family behind in Delhi and as tension mounted, I often wondered what was lying in store for all of us who were in Pakistan. Somehow I had a feeling the same fate which brought me in, would take me out too.

HERE ENDS MY DIARY ABRUPTLY AS I DID EVENTUALLY LEAVE KARACHI.

Index